A Pub On Every Corner

Volume Four: Scotland Road, Everton and Anfield

Freddy O'Connor

The Bluecoat Press

This book is dedicated to my wife Jean, two sons Paul and Stephen, daughter Helen and grandson Callum.

©2001 Freddy O'Connor

Published by The Bluecoat Press, Liverpool
Book design by March Design, Liverpool
Printed by GZ Ptintek SAL

Front cover Opie Street Vaults
Back cover Buffalo Arms, Gerald Street

All rights reserved. No part of this publication may be reproduced, stored in a retrieval system,
or transmitted in any form or by any means, electronic, mechanical,
photocopying, recording or otherwise, without prior permission from the publisher.

ISBN 1 872568 65 3

Acknowledgements

Thanks to: Harold Andrus (research and information), Jackie Ball (photograph), Rob Brennan (information), Frank Carlyle, Central Library (research and information), Ronnie Challinor (information), Community Services Department, Merseyside Police (information), Crosby Library (research and information), City Engineer's Department (photographs), Frank Dugan (photograph), Christopher Dudley (photograph), Ronny Formby, Scottie Press (information), Tony Jordan (photograph), Mick Keegan (information), Liverpool Daily Post & Echo (photographs), Liverpool Records Office (research and information), Jimmy O'Dowd (information), Olympia Hotel (information), John O'Brien (feature), John Page (information), HB Priestley, The National Tramway Museum (photograph), Edward B Senar (feature and information), Frank Stafford (feature and photograph), Bill Stephens (information), Mike Taylor (information and photograph), Tetley Walker Estates Department (photographs and information), John Wheatland (information), Fr Tom Williams, St Anthony's Church (information), Bill Wordsworth (photograph). A special thanks to my Dad, also my brothers Frank, Ray and Peter.

Special thanks also to John McKeown for research material and photographs.

Introduction

This publication primarily covers Scotland Road, the large Everton district of Liverpool and also Anfield, Tuebrook and West Derby. When pubs are not listed in any particular era, it means that they were closed but may have reopened as a pub, or other business, at a later date, whereas pubs listed 1964 or 1970 were open during those years but have since been demolished. Modern pubs, unless relevant to the text, have been omitted.

Demolition of insanitary property has been going on in Liverpool's central areas since the 1860s and, wherever it occurred, plenty of licensed premises have always been affected but were generally the last to be demolished. This is well-illustrated in the Everton area, especially in the 1960s and 70s, when mass clearances of whole communities left lone pubs which sometimes remained open. One reason is that in 1970, Liverpool City Council had an agreement with the Liverpool and District Brewers' Association to safeguard as many pubs as possible in areas of redevelopment (see Valley Public House). Before and after that agreement, money was the main reason for this delay, as the following report by the Medical Officer of Health, 1912, indicated:

'The Medical Officer feels constrained to refer to the question of the licensed premises upon these areas and to urge that, in no instance, should these premises be excluded in dealing with the areas. The Medical Officer is fully aware that the cost of previous schemes has been greatly increased by the large amount of compensation paid for licensed premises but, at the same time, the advantages to the district from the reduction in their numbers are so great that it would be a misfortune to depart from the previous practice.

The committee has never had occasion to regret the adoption of this course in areas conspicuous for their extreme squalor and poverty and it is in these very areas, that such large sums of money are expended in these premises. Indeed, one firm, whose extensive ownership entitles its views to consideration, stated that a public house in such a situation 'is situated in perhaps the best neighbourhood for the public house trade in all of Liverpool' and occupies 'a particularly commanding position and the people were of the right sort, from the publican's point of view, as customers.'

Without in any way contesting this view, it appears that the best interests of the public health would be served by pursuing the course of removing these houses, notwithstanding the amount of money involved.

As explained in *A Pub on Every Corner, Volume 1* (Liverpool city centre), after an Act of Parliament of 1830, beer houses flourished in all the older parts of the town. Many simply traded in one room of the house, others in cellars. Confusion was rampant over one particular phrase in the licence of these beer houses. Part of the formal wording on the licence issued to such establishments gave rise to misapprehension, because it stated that various drinks were 'to be drunk on the premises'. However, to the ignorant (or crafty) licensees's summoned for 'permitting drunkeness' would argue that 'to be drunk on the premises' meant literally what it said! During the Victorian years, arguments galore over this phrase occurred in the Magistrates Courts, until a simple change to the wording changed the appropriate phrase to "to be consumed on the premises', still in use today.

Abbreviations used in the book:

BH	Beer House
PH	Public House
SD	Spirit Dealer
SV	Spirit Vaults
WSD	Wine and Spirit Dealer
WSM	Wine and Spirit Merchant
WSV	Wine and Spirit Vaults

Byrom Street Area and Scotland Place

The route from Dale Street, via Byrom Street, led northward from the city centre into Scotland Road. Byrom Street was originally known as Towns End Lane, from the days when Dale Street marked the end of the town. Later, it became known as Dog Kennel Lane, from the neighbouring kennels which belonged to the Corporation and supported a pack of hounds. Today, Byrom Street is part of a widened main thoroughfare, in and out of the city centre and is unrecognisable from its pre-1970s state.

The land on the whole length of the east side, from Hunter Street, was built on in the 1960s, as the City College of Technology and now forms part of the John Moores University. Only one building of the old property remains on the whole of its 331-yard length on the west side; a one-time pub, from over twenty that formerly stood there. It was known for many years as the Pie Shop, which was actually its name in the 1890s (Palmer's Pie Shop: Beer House & Eating House). It remained unnamed as a Beer House until the premises were rebuilt in the 1960s, when it was designated the Byrom, although still referred to as the Pie Shop.

After opening and closing on a number of occasions in the 1980s, an unsuccessful name change occurred in the early 1990s to Flash Harry's, which has now ceased trading and the pub has remained closed for a number of years, to date.

Above is a general view of Byrom Street from the 1920s, the Grapes Inn is on the left, at the time the manager was Arthur John Blakeway. Beyond the adjoining block is St Stephen's Church, 1870, which replaced an earlier church consecrated in 1792. This was located lower down Byrom Street, near the junction of Shaws Brow (later William Brown Street). The original chapel opened in 1722, as a meeting place for dissenters. Before becoming a place of worship, this site was originally a barn belonging to Townsend House.

The adjoining shops were: at number 62, Edward Banner, Chemist, at 60, Harry Bilton, Tobacconist, at 56-58, Mrs Annie Roberts, Newsagent, Town Sub Post and MO Office and at 54, Stephen Crute, Hairdresser.

About the time this was photographed, the squalid surroundings included court property, landing houses and narrow terraced streets, all of which were cleared to make way for one of the new, municipal schemes to replace slum property, Gerard Gardens. Although a great improvement on earlier-style tenements and despite the term 'Gardens' being a most inappropriate epithet, similar schemes during the 1920s and 30s rapidly appeared in various parts of Liverpool and were generally referred to as, 'walk-up flats'.

The majority of walk up flats, despite becoming established communities, are now mainly cleared. Gerard Gardens was demolished in the 1980s. (see Dart Public House, Great Crosshall Street, page 53)

The following six pubs were on Byrom Street.

East Side

Clayton

Formerly at 18 Byrom Street and 1-3 Clayton Street (abolished). , The pub was named after the street in the 1930s. It was earlier called the Angel, and pre-1890s the Westmoreland House, and pre-1860s, the Old England (probably an earlier structure at 16 Byrom Street).
The adjoining shop was Avery's, with another business, Frederick Dickinson Brush Works, established 1839, advertised above the shop. Photographed during the 1920s when managed by Harry Edgar Walker. Listed 1964.

Byrom Arms

A large corner pub, formerly listed at 32-34 Byrom Street and 2-4 Hunter Street. Photograph from 1912 when run by George Henry Allen, with adjoining Cocoa Rooms just visible. The pub replaced an earlier 1870s structure named Brunswick Buildings, part of which housed a Spirit Vaults and a Wine & Spirit Dealer. Listed 1964.
Over a span of years, Hunter Street once contained some 16 pubs and a number of breweries, including a former well-known local brewer, James Mellor, whose business was established in the 1820s. Originally numbered at 14-22 and then at 16-24, it traded until 1946, when taken over by Higsons. Surprisingly, for many years the name Mellors continued to be displayed on the pubs. Higsons Brewery, in Stanhope Street, remained in business until 1990 and has since reopened as a brewery once again.
Hunter Street is now unrecognisable from its former narrow status, currently a wide thoroughfare, sweeping eastward from Byrom Street to Islington.

Grapes Inn

Formerly at the junction of Byrom Street and Gerard Street (abolished), this pub was a Beer House pre-1930s. Photographed in 1908, when the licensee was Henry J Mercer. Premises closed in the 1950s.
Police Report 1903: Permitting drunkenness, dismissed.

Dunbar Castle

Situated at 72-74 Byrom Street, on the corner of Circus Street (abolished). Pre-1890s it was called the Circus Vaults and pre-1860s, the Byrom Arms. The pub was probably renamed after a proprietor of the 1890s - John Dunbar. The adjoining shop was listed to John Peck & Co Ltd, Butchers Outfitters, who also had the adjoining former dwelling house in Circus Street, probably as a stores/warehouse. The shop later became the once well-known Army and Navy Stores. Photographed in 1912, when the manager was Joseph Brown. Premises closed in the early 1960s.
Police Report 1900: Serving drink to a drunken man, dismissed.

West Side

Berry's Crown Inn

Formerly at number 57 Byrom Street. Listed as a Beer House pre-1920s, and United Distilleries Co, pre-1890s. The adjoining building belonged to a Manufacturer of Women's Overalls for Factory and Domestic Wear. Photograph from the 1920s. The name, Berry's, refers to William Berry, licensee from 1921-1930s, in all probability the man standing with his daughter in the doorway. The premises was known locally as Tom Snuff's. Listed 1964.

The Swan

Listed at 73 Byrom Street and 81 Great Crosshall Street, closing c 1930. The site then became used for municipal housing, Fontenoy Gardens, since demolished and the land has been landscaped. The sign outside the premises on a trestle reads: 'Steam roller at work'. Photographed approximately 1908, when the manager was Francis McHugh.

The following pubs were located east of Byrom Street.

Beer House

A typical, nondescript Beer House, so common in the older parts of pre-First World War Liverpool. One of an original nine pubs in Gerard Street, number 12, at the junction with Gregory Place. Photographed in the 1890s, when the licensee was Susannah Swanson, most likely the lady standing in the doorway with her children. Licence revoked by 1905. Listed to a grocer in 1908.

Duck House

Listed at 53a Gerard Street and 1 Bennett Street. Pre-1880s this was a Wine & Spirit Vaults, probably named after the licensee, John Duck, also a brewer, when photographed approximately 1904. Like several pubs of the time, it closed in the early years of the 20th century.

Police Report 1898: The division wall in this house is only four and a half feet high. Also, from 1902: Selling drink to a child under 14 years, dismissed. Notice of objection.

The Harlequin

Located amongst a maze of streets at number 11 St Stephen's Street and 10a Hunter Street. The premises was listed in the 1820s, named the Rising Sun in the 1840s, becoming the Harlequin by the 1880s.

Large lettering states the manager's name as Morton, no doubt the man in the picture, whose full name was William Ellerton Morton, licensee from 1905-1918. It closed in the 1920s. Another pub of this vicinity was the Dreadnought, situated in Cuerdon Street (abolished). It was not named after the famous

Below is a view showing the houses of Gerard Street in the 1920s, when the Duck House had become a corner shop which, coincidentally, belonged to the grandfather of a friend of mine, Peter Santangeli, whose surname is shown faded over the shop. As his name indicates, he is of Italian descent. At this time, east of Byrom Street was Liverpool's Italian quarter, although no trace now remains.

class of battleships, the first of which was launched in 1906. It dates from the 1860s and the name, Dreadnought, was the trade name for a cloth used for thick coats for stormy weather.

Police Report of 1892: The house is licensed as no 3 Cuerdon Street, but the only entrance in Cuerdon Street to the licensed premises is through a yard door.

This picture, taken in the 1950s, is of Scotland Place (abolished), which separated Byrom Street from Scotland Road. Three pubs can be seen in this photograph, centre right is the Dunbar Castle, on the left is the Morning Star and adjoining the Irish Depot, is the Birmingham Arms, alongside a drinking fountain, also featured.

On this site stood the old Porter Brewery, once the largest in Liverpool, described in *A Pub on Every Corner, Volume One*.

Scotland Place is a perfect example of how premises changed by name and numbering, also reflecting the difficult task of locating pubs from the 19th century.

The following list features public houses during the 1830s, then the same location in the 1890s and indicates how, during a span of 60 years, the numbers and some of the names were completely different. Compare them over a span of six decades. Some of the pubs remained standing until the 1960s.

1830s	1890s
Beer House and Eating House (8)	listed as Boot and Shoemaker (15)
Edinburgh Arms (9)	Green House (17)
Regent Tavern (10)	Liver Vaults (19)
Wine & Spirit Vaults (12-13)	Old Warehouse Public House (30-32)
Earl of Chester (later Royal Oak) (15)	Morning Star (24, 26 and 28)
Cabbage (later Old Cabbage) (20)	Old Rum Barrel (16)
Birmingham Arms (earlier Punch Bowl) (21)	Birmingham Arms (14)
Duke of York (22)	listed to a Pawnbroker (12)
Cumberland House (25)	listed to a General Dealer (6)
Spirit Vaults (27)	Grapes (2)

This view of Scotland Place is from 1860. Renumbering had occurred by then, with the building displaying the name Hooton situated at the junction of Circus Street, a Spirit Vaults, then at number 2. The licensee's full name was Luke Foster Hooton.

Adjoining number 4 was a watchmaker, listed to Joseph Bretherton, at 6 was James Hodson, Provision Dealer, at 8, John Forsyth, Stationer, at 10, Thomas Hegarty & Co, Butter Salesman (note the butter barrels outside the premises) and at 12, John Empson, Pawnbroker.

The sign on the left was Gowan H Corless, Painter, next to the Royal Oak, shortly to be renamed the Morning Star.

All the property on this view was demolished long before the previous photograph was taken.

The following are three of the former pubs of Scotland Place:

Liver Vaults

The Liver Vaults was at 19 Scotland Place and earlier at number 10. A magnificent structure built in the latter part of the 19th century, replacing the Regent Tavern at the junction of Addison Street, aptly named as the Liver bird was the trademark of Robert Blezard, brewer, whose family owned the pub. Elizabeth Blezard was the licensee of the nearby Old Warehouse Public House. (see Brewery Public House, Scotland Road)

Photographed approximately 1905, when the manager was John Joseph McDowell, the premises closed in the 1930s.

The adjoining shop, just visible, was occupied by the Dublin Tailoring Company, Tailors.

Eight pubs once stood on Addison Street which, in the 1600s, was named Sick Man's Lane, or Dead Man's Lane, originating from the practice of transporting plague victims from the town and placing them here in fever sheds. The location, in that period, was just beyond the edge of the old town. Victims were also interred nearby. In 1651 alone, some two hundred victims were buried here.

The horrendous number of deaths can be illustrated by an incident from about 1850. During excavation work for sewers, quantities of human bones were discovered by the navvies, who sold them by the bushel to marine store dealers, until they were stopped by the authorities.

The Old Cabbage

Listed at 16 and earlier at number 20 Scotland Place at the junction of Feather Street. To the east stood Richmond Row. As previously explained, this pub retained its original name until closure.

A sign reading Gerraghty's Vaults, probably referring to the owner can be seen. (The Waterloo, Dock Road, also displays this name). Photograph from the 1890s, when managed by Richard C Williams. Not listed 1940s.

Morning Star

Listed at 24-28 and earlier at number 15 Scotland Place. A well-known pub of its day, although a little confusion arises as to the origin of its name. It was called the Earl of Chester in the 1840s but, in a report about the pub in 1888, it was claimed that it was upwards of a hundred years old and called the Royal Oak. This name change only occurred in the late 1850s, after renumbering. It is known that during the 1860s the pub was extended (or probably rebuilt) and renamed the Morning Star, keeping the same name until closure, and was known locally as Blood's.

It was the last pub to be demolished on Scotland Place in the early 1960s. Photographed in the 1890s when the licensee was Felix Byrne.

The following is from 1888 concerning the Morning Star Public House:

'I remember a few years ago dropping into a Liverpool music hall, just as a Negro entertainer came on stage. He turned out to be a rather clever fellow but the only part of his business which I recall, was a song; something in the strain of the 'Cruise of the Calabar'; he set sail from somewhere in the neighbourhood of Boundary Street and, after a stormy passage down Scotland Road, during which he collided with every public house on the route - he mentioned their names - his craft ultimately, 'struck in a thousand pieces, right agin the Morning Star'. From this time, I noticed that a good many Irish-American, West African, Scotland Road Negroes, in the music halls and elsewhere, found the Morning Star a very prolific subject for fun and I made a special pilgrimage there, to satisfy my curiosity. I found it an imposing-looking place, though located in a roughish neighbourhood. There was a lot of gilt and glitter on the outside and a good many people hanging over the counters, inside. I stepped in and found Mr P Byrne, the renowned 'Dandy Pat', talking politics like a book. I tasted some of his whisky: it was Irish you know, real Irish you know! And over one or two glasses of 'DD', I heard plenty to amuse and instruct. Afterwards, I took an interest in the establishment and, although I had not visited the place for several years, I was surprised when I saw, a few days ago, an advertisement to the effect that the hotel was for sale, this set me thinking and I made a few enquiries in the matter.

It is now very nearly twenty years since Mr Pat Byrne became tenant of the Morning Star, at which period the house was owned by the mother of the present landlord, who, by the way, is a Conservative City Councillor. Dandy Pat is said to have expended considerable sums on the general improvements and extension of the house. The lease expires shortly, and the establishment has been thrown onto the market. It is said that Mr Byrne has offered to buy the house at a reasonable valuation, or to continue his tenancy at an equitable rent, but the purchase price, and the rent demanded, seem to preclude the possibility of the two parties arriving at a satisfactory settlement. The Morning Star, originally known upwards of a hundred years ago, as the Royal Oak, is one of Liverpool's oldest public houses, and it is asserted that the present Royal Liver Friendly Society originated in its parlours.'

This society, from its humble beginnings, grew nationwide and its headquarters in Liverpool's most prestigious waterfront location, the Royal Liver Building, still houses the society.

Shortly after the article was written, Dandy Pat died, aged forty-five, and a committee was set up to erect a drinking fountain in his memory. Strangely, the Health Committee did not approve of it and the Council had to force them to sanction it.

When it was finally erected on Scotland Place, in 1892, facing the Morning Star, the opening ceremony took place with the Health Committee executives still firmly against it, as this closing column from the Liverpool Review of 1892 reveals:

'Thus it is clear that Mr B Smith, and other members of the Health Committee, are determined to fight the Byrne memorialists to the last gasp. The City Council forced them to give permission for the erection of the fountain: it will now be necessary presumably for the Council to force them to accept it on behalf of the Corporation. Mr Byrne was a good and worthy citizen, in many ways. It is monstrous that a monument to commemorate his good deeds - approved by the Council - should be thwarted by Mr JB Smith and a mere handful of his fellow cronies.'

Like thousands of his fellow countrymen, Pat Byrne arrived in Liverpool penniless as a youth, first working on the docks, then, through a thrifty nature and careful living from his meagre wages, he eventually distinguished himself by becoming a philanthropist, local councillor, benefactor of the poor and victualler.

Before managing the Morning Star, he was licensee of the Green House at 17 Scotland Place. When established at the Morning Star, he also acquired a pub in Birkenhead, the Royal Rock Hotel, Bedford Road, Rock Ferry.

Patrick Byrne was the only publican in Liverpool known to have a monument erected to him. His popularity can well be illustrated by his funeral. It is recorded that over thirty thousand people walked behind the coffin after the service at St Joseph's Church, Grosvenor Street, to the Prince's Landing Stage, for shipment to Dublin. The procession was also followed by the Lord Mayor's carriage and all the public buildings in the city flew their flags at half-mast.

He was buried in Ferns, in his native Ireland. Incidentally, his nickname of Dandy Pat was due to his somewhat eccentric dress. He often wore a sealskin waistcoat and white top hat.

After Patrick Byrne's death, the pub was run by his cousin, Felix Byrne for a few years, before moving the short distance to manage number 12 Scotland Road, My Uncles Vaults (page 45). Although, somewhat confusing, a Felix Byrne is listed as a servant in Pat Byrne's will. His charitable nature can be revealed by the following extracts from his will, which also indicates the strong Catholic community of the Scotland Road area.

RC Bishop £200.
Rev Henry Roberts of St Joseph's - £50.
Rev Henry Roberts for the poor of the parish - £25.
Rev Henry Roberts for the benefit of the schools attached to St Joseph's Church - £50.
Rev Father Newsham of St Joseph's £50.
To the Rector, or Head Priest, of St Anthony's RC Church, for the benefit of the poor of St Anthony's district - £25.
To the Rector, or Head Priest, of the following RC Churches in Liverpool, respectively named: Holy Cross, All Souls (Collingwood Street) and Our Lady of Reconciliation (Eldon Street), the sum of £25 each for the poor of the district attached of such churches.
To the Rector, or Head Priest, of Holy Cross, for the benefit of the children of the school attached - £25.
To the Superioress of the Sisters of Charity in Everton Crescent - £50 for her own use.
To the Superioress of the Little Sisters of the Poor, Belmont Road, Liverpool, the sum of £50 for her own use.
To the Reverend William Dubberly, of the Church of St Francis

Xavier, Liverpool, the sum of £20 for his own use.

To the Reverend Jeremiah Dowling, of St Anthony's RC Church, Liverpool, the sum of £50 for his own use.

To each of the persons who, at my death, shall be servants or employees of mine, a legacy of £5 and, in addition, the further sum of £5, for every complete year that he or she has been in my employ or service.

To the Reverend Father Marshall, or the Priest in charge of the Parish in which Ferus Village, near Gorey County of Wexford in Ireland - £50 for the benefit of the poor of the said village.

To the said Father Marshall, or Priest in charge of the said Parish last named, the sum of £10 to be spent in a treat at Christmas for the schoolchildren of the said village and to the said Father Marshall, or Priest in charge - £50 for his own use.

To James Doyle and his sister Eliza - £25

To my housekeeper, Mrs Murphy, in addition to any legacy received as my employee, a further £25.

To my servant, Patrick Finnegan, in addition to any legacy received as my employee, a further £10.

To James Hamner, a little boy now living with me - £30.

To the Treasurer of the Seaman's Orphanage, Liverpool - £20.

To my servant, Felix Byrne, in addition to any legacy received as my employee, a further £25.

John Neill, of Woodview Terrace - £60.

To my sister-in-law, Mrs Byrne - £250, to her son John, the sum of £250, to my niece, Lizzie Hamner - £250, to my niece, Alice Hamner - £250.

Byrne Drinking Fountain

This picture, showing the fountain circa 1904, with a group of shoe-black boys, some in their bare feet. Note the large letters spelling the name of the Morning Star in the background. Taken from a different angle, this shot makes the pub look much larger than the previous photograph, from the 1890s.

The fountain remained until the 1970s and was then moved to Pownall Square. However, after being vandalised during the 1980s, it disappeared. During the 1990s Mike Kelly formed the Dandy Pat Memorial Project Committee and, along with other enthusiasts, discovered the plinth of the fountain in a yard owned by the council.

After restoration by stonemasons, the plinth is back in its rightful place, amongst the Scotland Road community, and now stands in the grounds of St Anthony's church.

The official unveiling took place on 14 April 2000, and was attended by many dignitaries, including special guests - Frances Moore and John Furlong, descendants of Patrick Byrne who came over from Ireland for the ceremony. It is hoped that bridges can be built between the local community and that of Ferns, County Wexford, Ireland.

Scotland Road

A rare view of Scotland Road from 1844. The outstanding church on the right was a Scotch Kirk, St Peter's. It opened in 1843 and, somewhat strangely, only survived until 1849, when another church was consecrated on the same site - St Matthew's.

The reason for its short existence was because the church of St Matthew's, in Plumbe Street, off Tithebarn Street, was due to be demolished as part of a scheme for the construction of a railway station. After a considerable amount of litigation connected with its demolition, the site of the Scotch Kirk in Scotland Road was bought by the Lancashire and Yorkshire Railway Company and given to the Rev Dr Hillcoat, in lieu of St Matthews, Plumbe Street.

A limited view of St Anthony's Chapel can be glimpsed beyond this church, together with the Wesleyan Association Chapel. This chapel survives to date, albeit having undergone extensive alterations. In 1912 a licence was issued to convert the premises into a cinema - the Derby Picturedrome. This remained open until 1960 and the building is currently in use as a funeral parlour.

Note what appears to be a water pump in the middle of the road. One of the houses centre right was listed to Owen Elias, a Welsh builder who had settled in Liverpool and was responsible for building numerous terraced streets throughout the city, particularly in this area, Everton, Toxteth and Walton. Jacob's Biscuit Manufacturers was later built on this site.

Over the centuries, the majority of towns and villages throughout the country had stone crosses and Liverpool was no exception; a number of them existed in the old town. They were often used in conjunction with markets and became important landmarks.

A cross was located in Scotland Road - the White Cross, also known as the Great Cross and Allan's Cross, referred to as early as 1300. It was located approximately by the present Hopwood Street, although at that time the road was unnamed and was probably no more than a primitive narrow footpath.

For centuries the land hereabouts was known as the Town Field, a section of which was named the Breckshoots. The cross marked the northern limit of the Breckshoots. Another cross, the Everston Cross, sometimes referred to as the Little Cross, or Overston Cross, marked the southern boundary and was located on the west side of Bevington Hill. The last reference to the White Cross appears to be in 1821, where it is shown on a map as the, 'Remains of an Ancient Cross'. It is known that, in 1771, the thoroughfare was widened, when it became one of Liverpool's two turnpike roads, the route going through Walton, Burscough, Preston, then Lancaster and finally reaching Scotland, hence its name.

The northern end of the road, from about Mile End, was originally named New Scotland Road. This was when it was still mainly a tranquil country retreat for the town's more well-to-do citizens; residing in semi-rural splendour until approximately 1830, before fleeing the advancing tide of bricks and mortar.

The road was widened again and steadily became built up northwards from 1803. Numerous shops, pubs, houses and a variety of businesses and industries ended its existence as an exclusive residential area. The 'new' epithet was dropped around 1840.

In the early 19th century it was fashionable to name streets after celebrated public figures. Examples around Scotland Road include Wellington, Horatio, Great Nelson, Collingwood and Ellenborough. However, not all the people given this honour were so widely known.

Meadow Street, off Rose Place, was named after William Meadows, who resided in the street. He was born in 1732 and, like Henry VIII, married an amazing six times. His first wife, whom he wed in 1755, lived just two years. A year later he married his second wife, who lived for twenty years and bore him nine children. After her death, with what seemed like indecent haste, he remained a widower for a mere month before his next marriage, which lasted two years. His fourth spouse was married to him for eighteen years, before she, too, passed away. After nine months a widower, he married his fifth wife - this union lasting eight years. Not one to relish the single state, in June 1807, at the age of 75, after mourning for just six weeks, he married his sixth wife. Upon hearing of his sixth marriage, a local man remarked, "What an extraordinary run of luck some men have!" He did not specify whether he meant good or bad luck!

Arguably the most well-known thoroughfare in Liverpool, Scotland Road, is sadly nowadays a mere shadow of the former close knit community which once lived there. The area suffered terrible damage during the Second World War and then along came the planners and the construction of the second Mersey Tunnel in the mid 1960s, which destroyed a large portion of the road and district.

Many of the people born there, wherever they are living now, will hold cherished memories, both good and bad, happy and sad, of this unique neighbourhood. A wealth of stories could be told, particularly of the many characters of the vicinity who are sadly no longer with us.

Pre-Second World War days, it was not all wine and roses, as some former residents would have us believe. Pub brawls were common, particularly on Saturday nights. An old tradition, now lost in history, was that when a fight between two individuals was about to happen in one of the pubs, it would often be put off until the next morning.

Then, in such places as the Lockfields, by the Leeds/Liverpool Canal, the fight would take place, in front of an eager audience. Once the fight was over, the combatants would shake hands and that would be the end of the matter.

The old lock up, in Rose Place, was always full on Saturday nights, yet some of the old policemen of D Division, if called out to a pub fight, would often sort out the disagreement themselves up the nearest entry - an accepted, if unauthorised, practice of the day.

Such spectacles were a legacy from centuries past when, in towns and villages throughout the country, pugilistic combats were a common occurrence. Before 1812, for example, open land on the east side of Lime Street, known as Waterworth's Field, on the site where Gloucester Street was later built, was used for just such encounters. A contemporary writer expressed his disapproval of such goings on:

'In the fields thereabouts, disgraceful exhibitions of brutality took place in cock-fighting, dog-fighting and pugilistic encounters, when the roughs of the town, who were fond of assembling there, had their little differences to settle.'

The poverty which still abounded in the area before the Second World War is, to some, a vivid, living memory. However, in Victorian times, the extent of the squalor and destitution was on an altogether more horrific scale. Recreation was virtually unknown. In fact, the public house was one of the few places, open to the poor, in which they could escape the wretched conditions of their hovels. With so many pubs crammed within one area, disorder and violence, fuelled by alcohol, became part and parcel of the daily life of the impoverished population.

The following two extracts give an indication of that life. The first is from the 1880s:

'There is probably more drunkenness in Scotland Road public houses on Saturday night, than in any other single thoroughfare in the city. One reason for this is, of course, that the road contains, in proportion to its length, a larger number of public houses than any other in Liverpool. In any one of these houses, it would be quite safe to say that an observant visitor might depend upon finding two thirds of those present, evidently under the influence of drink and a certain number, positively and obviously drunk - obviously so, at any rate, to anyone but a barman, or his employer.

This naturally leads to scenes of violence of which, however, the public hears very little, thanks, apparently, to a benevolent conspiracy on the part of the publicans and the police to spare their feelings. Sometimes the violence ends in death and then the matter cannot be hushed up, or shuffled out of sight, but results in a trial such as we had at the Assizes last week. In this case there was a drunken brawl in a Scotland Road public house on Saturday night, the 13th March, in the course of which, one of the men was fatally stabbed and another injured.

The man charged with the offence said that he had used the knife in self-defence, after being brutally ill-treated and, on this plea, which was endorsed by a judge, he escaped with a verdict of manslaughter and the sentence of six months' hard labour.'

Ten years later, the following article appeared in the *Graphic*:

'In the evidence given before the liquor commission, now sitting in the House of Lords, Liverpool came out particularly badly and an almost incredible tale was told by the chief witness of streets and slums peopled by drunkards, of women sodden in the public houses on Saturdays and merry drinking at home, from Saturday to Monday, of drinking and drunken children.

The worst of all the districts is said to be that through which Scotland Road runs and the slums and alleys of which abut upon that thoroughfare. The district itself was painted in the darkest colours and Scotland Road was held up to view as showing in its squalor and wretchedness, a vivid picture of the curse. An unprejudiced observer of Scotland Road might well ask himself whether it was not rather a cause.

The murky alleys, the roadways stinking with refuse, the broken-windowed, broken-doored houses, suggest the reflection that anyone whom poverty compelled to live there, might well get drunk as a periodical anaesthetic.

The houses are pigsties; the public houses are at least warm, well-lighted and comfortable; and although the attractions of beer are not very high in themselves, yet to a population which has no amusements beyond loafing and fighting, and no comforts beyond that of cuddling in rooms where the third plague of Egypt stalks unceasing, it must appear in the guise of something like a blessing.'

It is a fact that the road contained more pubs than any other in Liverpool; an incredible calculation that, over a period of time, approximately 110 separate pubs once lined the thoroughfare. It must also be remembered that many of the old beer houses, and even named pubs, were often omitted from lists in directories altogether, particularly in the early 19th century.

In the early 1820s, some 15 pubs were listed, including four in New Scotland Road, this figure rose to 29 by 1829 and, by the 1840s, over 40 existed. The saturation point was from the 1850s to the start of the 20th century, when anything from approximately 60 to around a 100 pubs were trading at any one time (albeit that some were short-lived).

The 20th century saw a gradual decline in this heavy concentration. At the time of the First World War, just over 40 pubs were open, falling to 30 just after the Second World War. Twenty-eight were still trading in 1964, diminishing to 16 by 1970. The unstoppable decline in the number of public houses along Scotland Road into the year 2001, leaves only four currently trading. I have included all the pubs which can be traced.

Most pubs in this, and other districts, were mainly frequented by people from a working class background. During the 1960s and earlier, one group of workers in particular was to be found in abundance in Liverpool pubs - the dockers.

Back in the 1930s, in pubs such as the Milton or the Wheatsheaf on Scotland Road, many an unemployed man would approach a friend or aquaintance who worked on the docks and ask what were his chances of getting a job down there. An informal word from his friend in the ear of a dock boss, usually meant that he got his chance - albeit only casual work. It was much appreciated, and no doubt a few bob changed hands in the pub, not to mention a drink or two!

However, the adage of the times - charity begins at home - was all too prevalent amongst the majority of dock workers. Members of entire families, from fathers to sons and grandsons, with the inclusion of cousins and in-laws, were employed from one generation to the next. Nepotism was rife along the waterfront in those dark days of want.

Nowadays few, if any, dockers frequent the remaining pubs on Scotland Road, or any other area for that matter, as their numbers have also undergone a dramatic decline.

West Side of Scotland Road

The following were, or are, on the west side of Scotland Road, (Numbers 1-75 were in Liverpool 3, numbers 77-443 were, or are, in Liverpool 5).

Britannia

Situated at number 13 on the corner of Scotland Road and Alexandra Pope Street, this pub was called the Waterloo in the 1820s, it became the Central Vaults about 1890, before receiving its final name c1908. When this picture was taken in 1912, Mrs Sarah Harrington Formby was the manageress.

The pub was a favourite watering hole for merchant seamen and known as Mary Kate's, after a former licensee. The adjoining shop belonged to James Bulloch, Outfitters. Listed 1970.

Milton

A Beer House until the 1860s (27 Scotland Road by 2 Court, 1840s) when named the Poets' Corner, being on the corner of Milton Street. By the 1890s, when it was possibly rebuilt, it was called the Clock and then finally became the Milton c1908, at 25-27 Scotland Road.

Photographed in the 1960s when the manager was George Quinn. Note that a section of the building had been turned into two shops: T Hackett, a Gent's Barber Shop and an Ice Cream Makers, run by the Chiappe Brothers. It was demolished as part of the second Mersey Tunnel scheme in the late 1960s.

There are a number of arched alcoves along the pub, which would probably have contained statues many years ago, most likely of poets, as its early name indicates. The pub and street were named after the English poet - John Milton (1608-74).

This was just one of a number of streets around Scotland Road named after English poets. Others included:

Joseph Addison (1672-1719)
Alexander Pope (1688-1744)
Ben (Benjamin) Jonson (1574-1637)
Geoffrey Chaucer (c 1340-1400)
John Dryden (1631-1700)
John Gay (1685-1732)

Juvenal Street and Virgil Street were both named after Roman poets. The name of the earliest known poet, Homer, reputed author of the *Iliad* and the *Odyssey*, is perpetuated in Great Homer Street. Very little is known of the poet, even the period of his life is not certain, presumed to be about 1250 BC.

Swan Inn

This pub, formerly at number 75 Scotland Road, was a Spirit Vaults pre-1880s and the George and Dragon pre-1860s. It was re-built at the junction of Arden Street and known locally as the Arden. This 1960s photograph was taken prior to demolition to make way for the Kingsway Mersey Tunnel. The three adjoining shops were: at 73, Leck Curphey Ltd, Engineering Merchant, at 69, Cassidy's Grocers Ltd and at 67, Ash & Son, Florist.

Rose Villa FC

Back row linesman - J Foley, J Hetherington, A Kelly, T Maddox, J Reddington, J Campbell, Team Secretary - F Stafford.
Front row referee - T Clisham, T Marsh, J Strode, H Marsh, T McCauley, D Kelly.

This view of the pub's football team from the early 1960s, was supplied by Frank Stafford, who recalled the following:

'Tim Clisham, who was a fully qualified referee, loved football so much he would rise very early on a Sunday morning and think nothing of marking out some ten pitches and then referee a match in the afternoon.

One hilarious incident happened on an exceptionally thick foggy Sunday morning. Braving the elements, Tim set off to the pitch in Woolton, carrying a bag of lime weighing about 56 pounds on his back. When the fog eventually lifted and the team came out to play, they all fell about laughing when one of the players shouted, "that's a big corner flag, Tim!" He had gone around a huge oak tree when lining the pitch!'

During this time, the pub was locally known as Josie's, after Josie McDermott, who ran the pub with her husband, Charlie, an uncle of the former Liverpool FC player, Terry McDermott.

Castle Inn

This was one of the earlier pubs on the road, located at 87 Scotland Road, on the corner of Wellington Street. In the 1820s it was called the Castle Inn North. This photograph is from the 1890s, when the manager was Edward Bayliff. The bar to the left was private, as written on the window; a normal practice of the day. The street names were displayed on the glass of the gas lamp. By 1908 the premises had been taken over by a Boot & Shoe Manufacturer.

Police Report 1900: Selling drink to a drunken man, 10/- plus costs.

One of the earliest licensees of this old inn was Robert Chambers, in the 1820s. Before acquiring the inn he was a coach driver and in those far off days he probably related the following story many times to his regulars, as they lounged in the bar.

During the early 19th century, the outskirts of Liverpool were infested with highwaymen, who either went about in bands, or singly, to rob horsemen, stop coachmen or even people on foot. Anyone out after nightfall could expect to be stopped and ordered to stand and deliver.

An affray took place at Everton Lane (Everton Road) opposite Mill Lane, in November 1812, that was characteristic of the time. This particular gang had been terrorising the outskirts for some time and the authorities were determined to capture them.

Five constables (dressed as civilians at that time, before the formation of the police as a body) were engaged to do the job. Robert Chambers was commandeered to drive a coach, drawn by four horses, to act as a kind of decoy. He drove along Vernon Hall Lane and Low Hill at a leisurely pace and on into Everton Lane. On reaching Mill Lane, five highwaymen fell into the trap and ambushed the coach. Wrenching open the door, they aggressively ordered the passengers out.

As previously agreed, one of the constables immediately alighted from the coach and was being searched by the ruffians, when the others sprang out and a general melée ensued. Pistols were discharged on both sides and one of the constables was severely wounded, and two of the thieves were also hurt. The other highwaymen managed to escape on foot, hotly pursued down the hill by the constables. They were finally caught in Folly Lane (later Islington).

The five men were tried the following year at Lancaster and each of them was found guilty and subsequently executed.

Old Black Bull Inn

This early view, clearly displaying the pub's name, is from the 1890s, when the licensee was Ann Rowlands, whose family ran the pub until the 1920s, when it was listed at number 127 Scotland Road.

To the left of the pub is an entrance to some court property (Oxley Court). Although nothing more than a narrow passage, the entrance was named Bull Entry. The adjoining shop to the right, showing the letters K I, belonged to the once well-known, King and Heywoods, Basket Makers established 1890s (see the photograph on the following page). Previously it was a large Drapers - William Morgan and Co.

The whole block was demolished and rebuilt just after the turn of the century. The rebuilt pub now has a date of 1905 on its facia and, due to the reconstruction, the pub was then renumbered at 145 Scotland Road.

The former passage, leading to the court property, remained as and was still referred to by its old name of Bull Entry. The whole block, situated between Hawley Street and Bevington Hill, stood until demolition as part of the Mersey Tunnel scheme in the late 1960s.

Police Report 1903: Selling drink to a drunken woman, bound over.

Awaiting Demolition

This is the block mentioned previously, looking south down Scotland Road, with Bevington Hill on the right. The Old Black Bull Inn can just be seen near the bus. The whole block was about to be demolished when this picture was taken in the late 1960s.

The shop that adjoined the Black Bull Inn - King and Heywood's, had moved shortly after the rebuilding, taking over a large portion of the same block higher up as far as the clock tower and was then listed as a Drapers & House Furnishers. King and Heywood's ceased trading in the 1930s.

By the early 1960s various different businesses had emerged as follows:

177a	Round Counter Snack Bar (Clock Tower section)
177	Harrops (Chemists) Ltd
175	Sheltons Painters & Decorators
173	Laurence Michaels Ltd, Ladies Outfitters
171a	R & N Samuels, Outfitters
171	Greenlees & Sons (Easiephit Footwear) Ltd
169	S Gordon & Co Ltd, Grocers
165 – 167	Lloyd's Retailers Ltd, House Furnishers
163	Walter Wood, Butcher
161	Scotland Road House Furnishing Co
159	Nathan Shieldhouse, Outfitter
157	Hill-Glover & Co, Fruit Merchants
155	John Gold, Jeweller
155	Arthur Newman, Optician
153	Town Sub-Post MO & Telephone Call Office
151	J Telford & Son Ltd, Confectioners
149	Edward Roberts, Tailor
147	Miss Winifred Coppack, Fruit Dealer
145	Black Bull Inn
143	Donald O'Williamson, Boot Dealer, Hawley Street

All these businesses had to look for new premises when the block was demolished in the late 1960s.

Mile End Vaults

Pre-1860s this pub was named the George and Dragon and was situated at 195 Scotland Road where it meets Mile End. During the early 19th century, when Scotland Road was still mainly rural, for some 40 years this old inn was at the northern limit of the road. Few buildings were located further north and, like the nearby Bevington Bush, was a popular meeting place for family picnickers on a walk out in the country. At that time, it had a reputation for selling scrumptious meat pies.

By the 1860s, the area had been transformed into a completely different, urban environment. The pub was probably rebuilt during this time and was renamed Mile End House, so called because it was exactly one mile from the Exchange (Town Hall) and it was listed at 197 Scotland Road and 43 Mile End. A Bent's house when photographed approximately 1960, at about which time it became known as Mile End Vaults. Listed 1964.

Plough Vaults

Located at 229-231 Scotland Road, at the junction of Hornby Street. Photographed in 1912, when the manager was George Francis Jarvis. Pre-1860s it was a Spirit Vaults. Listed 1964.
Police Report 1902: Selling drink to a drunken woman, bound over.

Bevington Arms

Listed at 259-261 Scotland Road and 39 St Martin Street, pre-1860s it was a Beer House. Note the unusually large side window on the first floor. It may well have been converted from an opening where a hoist would have been used to gain access to storage on the upper floors, many examples of which can still be seen around the town, particularly on three storey buildings.

Photographed in the 1920s, when the manager was Robert Johnson. The adjoining shop was a Boot and Shoe Dealer belonging to Harry Kendrew.

This pub was known locally as the Sweat Rag, from the sweat rags worn around the neck by the stokers and firemen of the old coal burning ships, who frequented the pub during the War and earlier. This nickname could have been equally appropriately applied to any pub in the vicinity, such was the huge number of men from the Scotland Road area serving in the Royal and merchant navies. Listed 1964.

The Ship

277 Scotland Road, on the corner of Wright Street. Pre-1880s it was named the Royal Oak, then it became the United Distilleries Co, Wine & Spirit Merchant, until it became the Ship at about the time of the First World War. Wright Street is the first street northward that leads into Scotland Road, all the other streets have been demolished at their junctions with the main road to form either the entrance, or the approaches, to the Kingsway Tunnel.

John Carroll was the licensee until just after the First World War, when he was succeeded by Mrs Mary Carroll, in the 1920s, when this photograph was taken. The adjoining building was the City of Liverpool Equitable Co-operative Society Limited. Listed 1964.

The Foot Hospital

This pub is situated at the junction of Silvester Street at number 291 Scotland Road. Originally a Spirit Vaults, it was then named the Grapes about the time of the First World War. However, it was known locally as the Foot Hospital and, as this 1994 view shows, the nickname had been adopted. During the 1990s the pub opened and closed several times and is currently closed (closed in the photograph).

I was informed that the nickname came about when a customer who had had too much to drink, fell over the steps of the pub and, on landing shouted, "Me foot's gone, take me to the foot hospital," or words to that effect. This simple, fleeting incident and remark were, for some reason, from that moment on, always associated with the pub and gave rise to a nickname that would stick. At the time in the 1930's, there was a foot hospital in the nearby Anfield area, as illustrated in this advertisement.

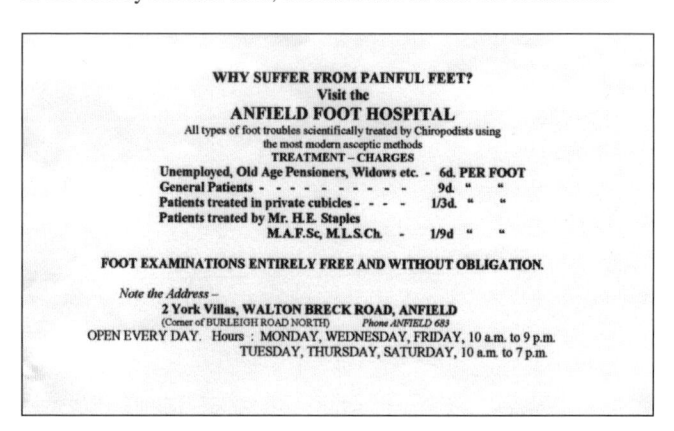

> **WHY SUFFER FROM PAINFUL FEET?**
> Visit the
> **ANFIELD FOOT HOSPITAL**
> All types of foot troubles scientifically treated by Chiropodists using the most modern aseptic methods
> **TREATMENT – CHARGES**
> Unemployed, Old Age Pensioners, Widows etc. - 6d. PER FOOT
> General Patients - - - - - - - - - - 9d. " "
> Patients treated in private cubicles - - - - 1/3d. " "
> Patients treated by Mr. H.E. Staples
> M.A.F.Sc, M.L.S.Ch. - 1/9d " "
>
> **FOOT EXAMINATIONS ENTIRELY FREE AND WITHOUT OBLIGATION.**
>
> Note the Address –
> **2 York Villas, WALTON BRECK ROAD, ANFIELD**
> (Corner of BURLEIGH ROAD NORTH)   Phone ANFIELD 683
> OPEN EVERY DAY. Hours : MONDAY, WEDNESDAY, FRIDAY, 10 a.m. to 9 p.m.
> TUESDAY, THURSDAY, SATURDAY, 10 a.m. to 7 p.m.

The Plough

View from the 1820s, showing Ye Olde Plough Inn situated close to Oxford Street North, later Silvester Street, when the northern end of Scotland Road was still mainly rural. It was named the Original Plough and numbered 283 New Scotland Road, in the 1840s, when the licensee was James Harrison.

This view features the same location as the Plough, between Silvester Street and Woodstock Street, in approximately 1950. The central building, the Plough Inn at 301 Scotland Road, together with the adjoining foundry, have been built on the site of the original inn. The licensee was Mrs Hannah O'Donoghue. The Globe can be seen to the extreme right.

Incidentally, adjoining Costigan's Grocery was a sack and bag merchants. Part of the building was taken up by the Lithuanian Social Club during the 1930s and 40s.

This photograph, from approximately 1970, shows part of the foundry demolished, with the remainder derelict. The building to the far left is the Grapes, at the junction of Silvester Street.

All the old property has since been demolished, leaving the Plough Inn in isolation, with its former nickname having been adopted as its proper name; the Widows. After a period of closure, the pub was finally demolished in 2000.

The Globe

Located at 309 Scotland Road and 41 Woodstock Street. Photographed in 1912, when the manager was Martin O'Toole. One of the adverts on the window was for Creaming Stout and note the unusual ball on the corner - not the usual Walker's sign, such as the one on the front but possibly relating to the pub's name, or earlier name, which was the Golden Ball pre-1860s. Known locally as Ted's prior to demolition, with the site currently landscaped. Listed 1970.
Police Report 1902: Selling drink to a drunken man, dismissed.

Westmoreland Arms

Situated at the corner of Westmoreland Place at 325-327 Scotland Road, this pub's nickname, Honky Tonk, was acquired in the 1980s, but, apparently, before the war, it was known as the Stone House. The adjoining shop belonged to Henry Appleton, Clog Maker. This 1950s photograph clearly displays the sign, O'Connor's Free House, although the pub was still named the Westmoreland Arms, with the licensee, Richard Hurley.

Westmoreland Arms

Here is the same premises in 1985, when the adjoining shop was vacant and in a dilapidated state of repair. This later opened as a pub named Dolly Hickey's. It was named after the mother of the last licensee of the Honky Tonk, who was well-known and one of the last barrow women of the area. Woodstock Gardens walk-up flats, now demolished, can be seen behind the pub.

On the pub's facia is written: 'Westmoreland Arms - one of Liverpool's oldest pubs, established 1740'. I have been unable to trace the pub as far back as this, although a brewer was listed in Westmoreland Place in 1818, possibly on this site.

The pub had opened and closed a number of times during the 1990s and whilst closed in 1996, it was gutted by fire, sadly resulting in the whole block being demolished in 1998.

Parrot Hotel

Open to date, at 347 Scotland Road where it meets Hopwood Street. Pre-1890s it was a Wine & Spirit Vaults and prior to 1860, it was named the Punch Bowl. Photographed in the 1950s, when managed by Frederick Haslam, it was known as the Blackpool House, as Caterall & Swarbrick's were Blackpool Brewers. In 1961, Northern Breweries took them over with 104 tied houses.

The adjoining empty shop and surgery, listed to John V Coghlan, has since been demolished, leaving the pub currently standing in isolation.

The Saddle Inn

Called the Saddle since the 1850s, this pub was located at 381 Scotland Road. Note the adjoining shop - the Spensobar, formerly well-known in the vicinity. The other shops are all empty, awaiting demolition, when photographed shortly before the pub closed in the early 1960s. It was then taken over by Coyne Bros Ltd, Funeral Directors, before being demolished in the late 1970s.

The Corner House

Located on the corner of Athol Street, at 393-395 Scotland Road, this was the last pub to remain open on the west side of Scotland Road. Listed as a Beer House pre-1870s, then named the Prince of Wales until approximately 1912. It was then unnamed until the 1930s, when it became Walker's Corner House. The word, Walker's, was dropped from the name in the early 1970s.

The adjoining shop was listed until the 1950s to William Williamson, Chemist. It has since been demolished, leaving the pub as the only remaining building and it is currently closed.

Note the barefoot children amongst the onlookers in this 1912 photograph, when the manager was Charles Brown.

Rotunda Vaults

Originally situated at 397 Scotland Road and 2 Stanley Road, from the 1850s it was known as a 'free and easy'. This term generally referred to a pub that engaged in concerts and sing alongs in the days before music licences.

Music halls were often part of, or adjacent to, such pubs and, by the 1860s, the premises was licensed as the Rotunda Music Hall.

The building was destroyed by fire in 1877 and in 1878 reopened as the Rotunda Theatre, a much larger building, as the new address indicates; 397 - 405 Scotland Road and 2 - 8 Stanley Road. During the 1890s it was also listed as a Billiard Rooms and American Bowling Alley. It was taken over in 1898 by Bents Brewery and then, after reconstruction in 1899, listed separately as: Rotunda Vaults at 397 Scotland Road and 2 Stanley Road, with the Rotunda Theatre listed at 397 - 405 Scotland Road. This view is from the early 20th century.

The licensee/proprietor, from the early 1860s until the 1890s, was Denis Grannell. He had also built and owned one of the country's most famous theatres; the Argyle Theatre, Argyle Street, Birkenhead (1869), as well as being the owner of a pub in the same street, the Argyle Hotel. Despite owning two theatres, he lived in a modest terraced house, at 46 Pluto Street, close to the Rotunda.

The Old Roundy, as it was known, was destroyed during the War, as was the Argyle Theatre. The site is currently a grassed open space, and this area is still referred to as the Rotunda today.

Brewery Vaults

Formerly at 417 Scotland Road (359 in the 1840s, when listed in New Scotland Road), a large public house, originally the last on the west side of Scotland Road. The adjoining structure, partly shown on the right, was the rather aptly-named, Liver Brewery, belonging to the Blezard family, whose name is on the window. Once a well-known Liverpool brewery, belonging to the Blezard family from the 1840s until 1921, it was then taken over by Walker Cain. It was later listed as the Castle Saccharine Works, Sugar Merchants. Throughout the 19th century, the Blezard family was linked with several breweries and public houses, for example the Liver in Scotland Place.

In the 1870s Robert Blezard lived at Breeze Hill House, at the boundary between Walton and Bootle. It was a large house, set in its own grounds, amongst similar detached villas and mansions tenanted by the middle classes of the period. The site of Breeze Hill House later became a school - the Bootle Secondary Grammar School, since renamed Hillside and open to date.

The property to the left, just showing the letters 'es' which represented the end of the word 'Carriages', belonged to a long-established Undertakers, John Waugh, still operational until the late 1950s.

Photographed in the 1920s, when the manager was Mrs Phoebe Rimmer. Known locally as the Bean House, the pub was demolished in the early 1960s and the site was grassed over.

Other pubs on the west side of Scotland Road.

1	Ormskirk Tavern, 1820s. Listed in New Scotland Road, before numerical changes, may have been at a different location.
7	BH, pre-1860s, then the Royal Prince Patrick, listed to a Clothier, 1880s.
9	Manchester and Liverpool Arms, 1850s.
17	BH, corner of Harrison Street, listed to a Pawnbroker, 1860s.
23	Masons Arms, pre-1840s, then a W & SV, junction of Milton Street, listed to a Flour Dealer, 1908.
27-29	Tradesman's Tavern. Pre-1840s, possibly on the site of the Milton (featured).
29	Cross Keys, 1820s. Listed in New Scotland Road before numerical changes, may have been at a different location.
33	Stag, pre-1880s, then a W & SV, junction of Cavendish Street, listed to the Liver Engraving Co, 1912.
35-37	North Tavern pre-1860s, junction of Cavendish Street, listed Dining Rooms, 1880s.
41	The Bull 1820s listed in New Scotland Road before numerical changes, may have been at a different location.
47	The Grapes, listed to a Currier 1860s.
49	The Grapes, pre-1930s, then the Pine Inn, at the junction of Edgar Street and Bevington Bush. Listed 1964.
51	Globe, pre-1840s, later a BH and Brewer and, from the 1880s the Coach and Horses, junction of Edgar Street/Bevington Bush. Listed to a Furniture Dealer 1912.

Police Report 1892: The back door of the shop adjoining opens into the yard of the public house, the backyard of which, opens into an enclosed entry, into which the back doors of four private houses open. When the entry door is closed, the police have no access to the rear of the licensed premises.

77-79	Coffee House, 1840s, then listed as Distillers and Rectifiers, junction of Arden Street. Number 79 listed to the Liverpool Tobacco Co, 1880s, 79-81 later a Pawnbrokers.
83	BH, listed to a Tea Dealer, 1860s.
85	Speed the Plough, pre-1840s listed before numerical changes, may have been at a different location.
103	Golden Ball pre-1860s, then the Globe, situated at the junction of Ellenborough Street. Listed to a Tobacconist 1908.

Police Report 1903: Supplying drink to a drunken man, dismissed.

111	W & SV, pre-1880s, listed by no 4 Court, then the Grove, at the junction of Maddox Street. Listed to the Singer Sewing Machine Co Ltd, 1908.

Police Report 1892: Permitting drunkenness, dismissed.

121	BH listed to a Tea Dealer 1880s.
161	Squirrel pre-1840s, listed before numerical changes, so may have been at a different location.
165	Gardner's SV, listed to a Grocer 1860s.
171	Rose and Crown, 163-175, listed as Drapers & House Furnishers by 1908, after rebuilding.
179	Travellers' Rest, known locally as the Red Brick, listed 1964.
187	BH, listed to a Pork Butcher 1860s.
203	Lord Nelson, listed by number 1 Court 1840s, until the 1890s, then named the Green Flag. Listed as Boots Cash Chemists by 1908.
245	BH, junction of Tenterden Street. Listed to a Grocer 1880s.
251-253	Crown and Anchor, not listed 1912.
261	SV 1850s, probably became amalgamated with 259-261.
271	Parkinson's SV, 1850s, then the Nile Tavern 1860s and finally the Grapes at 269-271. Listed to a Milliner 1920s.

Police Report 1892: Failing to admit the police to licensed premises, dismissed. And 1898: Selling drink to a drunken man, ten shillings and costs.

287	SV, pre-1890s, then British Workman Public House Co Ltd listed to a Tattoo Artist, by the First World War.
311	BH, listed to a Grocer 1860s.
335	Lathom Hotel, at 333-335 at the junction of Benledi Street, listed to a Draper 1920s.

Police Report 1892: Serving drink to a drunken man, 10/- and costs.

339	BH, listed to a Grocer 1908.
357	BH, junction of Doncaster Street. Listed to a Butcher 1880s.
369-371	BH & Brewer, listed to a Pork Butcher 1880s.

East Side of Scotland Road

It is generally accepted that Scotland Road had only been built up as far as Dryden Street, on its eastern side, by the 1830s. However, there was, in fact, some property already built further north, together with a number of streets either fully or partially built on, such as: Newsham Street, St James Street North (later Kew Street), Bostock Street, Dalrymple Street and Mould Street.

Included in this property were some courts and a number of pubs on the main road, which were amongst the earliest buildings to be demolished outside of the city centre.

The pubs were a Spirit Vaults at number 282, the Mariners, earlier the Windmill, at 284, a Spirit Vaults at 296a and a Spirit Vaults at 312, all cleared by the early 1840s and located around St Anthony's Church, before the numerical changes took place. With the completion of the road, between Dryden Street and just before St Anthony's Church, buildings which had already been built further north, then altered their numbers as featured.

The first large scale attempt to clear the dreadful slums east of Scotland Road commenced from the 1860s, when Cazneau Street was extended northward into Scotland Road. This scheme cleared many of these wretched dwellings and later part of the land was used to build the Victoria Square tenements.

Victoria Square Tenements

These huge, five-storey tenement blocks, consisting of 269 tenements and 12 shops, were built, in 1885, and won an architectural award for their advanced design when erected.

This was the second major scheme to combat the slums of Victorian Liverpool, the first being St Martins Cottages (see Silvester Street).

Located between Lawrence Street, Cazneau Street, Juvenal Street and McKee Street and originally consisting of five, five-storey blocks, they were described thus: 'On each landing sinks have been provided, as well as a laundry, with boiler and wash places, for the use of the tenants of four dwellings in common and there are also two WCs, each common to two tenements.'

This view of one of the blocks, is from McKee Street during demolition in 1966. The site is now obliterated as part of the surrounds of the Kingsway (Mersey Tunnel) entrance/exit.

A similar scheme was the near-by Juvenal Buildings (1890), made up of four blocks, three of which were four storeys in height, and one of three storeys, comprising 101 tenements in all.

The following were on the east side (Numbers 2-222 were in Liverpool 3 and numbers 224-484 were, or are, in Liverpool 5).

My Uncle Vaults

Listed at number 12 at the junction of Hare Place, (abolished). Pre-1860s named the Puncheon and Still. Photographed approximately 1912, when the manager was Felix Byrne, the name Scotland Road is written on the glass of the gas light. Premises changed names again about 1918 to the Munster Arms, until closure in the 1930s. It is then listed as a Pawnbrokers.
Police Report 1898: Permitting drunkenness, bound over.

Faugh a Ballagh

Situated at 40 Scotland Road and photographed in the 1890s, when the manager was Robert Rawlinson. As can be seen throughout this book, there were some very unusually named pubs in Liverpool but this must rank as the one of the strangest. It apparently derives from a Munster Irish Regiment, who were disbanded in 1916. Named the Dog and Partridge pre-1860s.

It was renamed the Shamrock about the turn of the century then, probably in an effort to keep trading, acquired the name, the Dog and Partridge, after the First World War. However, closure occurred in the late 1920s and it was listed as Dining Rooms in 1930. An adjoining pub, the Green Doors, can partly be seen. (see next view).

The entry at the other side of the pub led to some atrocious court property which stood between Gay Street and Ben Jonson Street (both abolished).

Police Report 1898: The sanitary arrangements at this house when visited were in a most unsatisfactory state, the seat and the basin of the WC being broken and the place in a filthy condition.

The Green Doors

This building at the junction of Gay Street was originally a pub: a Spirit Vaults pre-1870s, then the Green Doors, closing in approximately 1904. It was then taken over by a Bedding Manufacturers, before conversion into two shops. The former Faugh A Ballagh pub has just been demolished in this view and the coping stones are all that remain. This view from the late 1960s shows two shops at 42 and 42a shortly before demolition - Podestas Fish and Chip Shop and a General Store listed to E Byrne.

Bush Vaults

Listed at 56-58 Scotland Road and 2 Rose Place, this pub was a Brewery prior to 1880s, then listed as the New Inn and a Wine & Spirit Vaults until it became the Bush Vaults in the 1890s. It was known locally as Tom Feeney's, after a manager from the 1930s/1940s era. The adjoining shop was probably part of the pub pre-1890s, when it was listed at 56-64.

This photograph is from the late 1960s, shortly before it, and the comparatively modern houses behind it, were demolished.

The Market Hotel

Formerly at 166 Scotland Road, it was called the Market Vaults until the 1880s, then the Grove Hotel, before it received its final name, the Market Hotel. Flanked by a Confectioners on the left and Dining Rooms on the right when photographed around 1920. Tim Foley had just taken over as manager and had had his name painted on the window. He presumably changed the name from the Grove Hotel to Market Hotel.

Tim Foley remained as manager until 1931. He then became the manager of 63 Byrom Street, before taking over the Travellers Rest at number 179. The premises closed in the 1930s.

The Wheatsheaf

Situated between Lawrence Street and Horatio Street. 1840s it was a Victualler, Butcher and Cow Dealer at number 180. Named the Greyhound, 1860s-1880s, then the Wheatsheaf at 180-184.

This view features the name Finnegan's Wheatsheaf Inn. Patrick Finnegan was licensee from 1901-1905, then James Finnegan took over until 1914. Not listed 1940s. The property shown behind the gates adjoining the pub was formerly a slaughterhouse, the licence of which was revoked in 1912.

The Eagle Hotel

Situated at 202-204 Scotland Road and 1 Great Nelson Street. In this 1950s photograph it was a Threlfalls House and the licensee was Alexandra Morrison. It was known locally as the Nell, probably a short version of Great Nelson Street. It took the name 'Hotel' only since the 1940s, previously known simply as the Eagle, and pre-First World War, the Eagle Inn. Listed 1970.

Police Report 1892: Two doors of premises in Scotland Road open into yard of public house, by which persons could pass between without being observed by police.

The Eagle

A large pub at 220-222 Scotland Road and 2 Collingwood Street (abolished), it was named in approximately 1908. Previously listed as a Wine & Spirit Vaults, pre-1880s it was called the Northern Light.

It was managed by Walter Ernest Turner when this photograph was taken in 1912. It was listed as the Eagle Vaults at various dates.

All Souls Church

This view is of All Souls Church, formerly located in Collingwood Street, one of many Catholic parishes in the area.

By the 1830s, Collingwood Street had declined from a pleasant, rural, tree-lined street of cottages, to a filthy, court-ridden street, as the population began to explode at an unprecedented rate.

The street contained ten narrow sinews under the name 'buildings' such as Collingwood Buildings and Williams Buildings, which were simply courts under another name. There was also a Coddington Place and Roscommon Terrace, which may have been early terraced property.

By the 1860s, conditions had deteriorated to a level of squalor which is difficult to comprehend nowadays. Death, be it from famine, or the numerous associated illnesses suffered by the poor, was so common in the district, that there was literally no space for corpses awaiting burial. The poor who inhabited these tiny, cramped hovels, already disease-ridden and living in abject poverty, frequently had to contend with the bodies of dead relatives, awaiting burial.

Such was the deprivation of the times, that it was not uncommon for a woman to have to occupy the same bug-ridden bed as her dead husband, and vice versa.

With the massive influx of poor and often illiterate Irish migrants swelling the already overcrowded slums, the Scotland Road area gradually became an almost wholly Catholic ghetto. The intolerable situation that the poor endured even overrode religious bigotry, as Protestants, distressed by the deplorable situation around Collingwood Street, raised £4,970 to build a temporary morgue. This morgue eventually became a local parish church, aptly named All Souls, which opened on St Patrick's Day, 1872. During the first sermon, a Father Hogan spoke of the poverty of the area and referred to the common practice of the dead occupying the same bed as the living.

The building remained as the local parish church throughout those dark days and continued to serve the community through the two World Wars but, sadly, after nearly 100 years, the church was demolished, along with all the surrounding property, as part of the scheme for the second Mersey Tunnel.

Dryden Hotel

Situated at 272-274 Scotland Road and 2-4 Dryden Street, pre-1860s it was called the Boat Spirit Vaults, when it was at 250 (probably rebuilt).

A large flamboyant pub, which was photographed approximately 1912, when managed by Thomas Howard. The premises was long known locally as Tom Howard's, quite justifiably, as he was listed as manager from 1908 until just after the Second World War. The adjoining shop was listed to James Longworth, Watchmaker.

Police Report 1892: Permitting drunkenness, 4/6 and costs.

Jacob's Biscuits

Despite the huge number of pubs on Scotland Road, there was still room for the many other businesses which flourished over the years, Jacob's Biscuit Manufacturers probably being one of the best known. Opened by Captain Jacob, whose family were Quakers, in 1912, when this photograph was taken. The business eventually moved to Aintree Industrial Estate, where they remain to this day. The building shown here still stands, although having undergone various alterations over the years.

In the early days of the factory, no Roman Catholics were employed. Although this would be unacceptable in today's society, during the early 20th century it was quite common for firms to only employ either Catholics or Protestants, a practice illustrating the bitter sectarianism that once existed in Liverpool.

Eagle Vaults

This pub is still open to date and is located at 330-334 Scotland Road, at the junction of Penrhyn Street. This view is from approximately 1970, when it was an Ind-Coope house. The exterior appearance of the pub has altered little over the years.

Throstle Nest Hotel

This drawing is from approximately 1860 and shows the steps of the adjoining St Anthony's Church. The premises was then at 282a Scotland Road. Some 20 years earlier it was listed at 254, when it was sandwiched between number 13 Court and the Mariners Arms at 284. Listed nearby was a Spirit Vaults at 296a, near number 15 Court (see beginning of East of Scotland Road).

The trees fronting the premises, shown on this view, apparently contained cages of live throstles, hence the name.

Throstles Nest

Open to date, now at 344 Scotland Road, at the junction of Chapel Gardens (originally Chapel Walks North). The pub has a date of 1881 on its facade, although having the same number since the late 1860s, (possibly rebuilt in 1881).

Photographed in the 1970s when it was a highly decorative pub. In 1985 the premises closed for renovation. After reopening, it was named One flew over the Cuckoo's Nest, with the current sign displaying One Flew over the Throstle's Nest, although, presumably, it will still be referred to locally as the Throstles.

The adjoining shops were: Cousins, Confectioners, G King, Fishmonger and Tuebrook Cleaners Ltd. The last named pair of shops have now been converted into a Licensed Betting Shop.

Newsham House

A former Wine & Spirit Vaults at 350-352 Scotland Road and 2-4 Newsham Street, the photo featuring the pub before the First World War. The nickname of this pub is the Holy House, possibly due to its close proximity to St Anthony's Church. Another explanation is that a former manager supposedly would not allow bad language to be used in the pub. My personal opinion is that the nickname derives from the pub's structure, as the old photograph shows; the upstairs windows strongly resembling church windows. I wondered if the style of the windows indicated some connection with St Anthony's Church but, after talking to the Parish Priest, Father Tom Williams, it seems that there is none.

The manager, when photographed in 1908, was Lancelot Crookdale, a rather uppercrust name for the manager of a humble pub in Scotland Road during those days.

The house adjoining the pub, in Newsham Street, surprisingly avoided the bulldozer. The shop shown on Scotland Road was listed to WO Roberts, Saddler.

Newsham House

Showing the pub in the 1970s, when the unusual, arched windows had been replaced by more conventional ones. The other main difference is that only two doors, from an original four, were now in use.

The adjoining shop was then Joe Doyle & Son, Family Butcher. The block was demolished in 2001.

As an insight into the former squalor of the vicinity, this epitaph is from the vaults of St Anthony's Church. The priest was one of ten who died in 1847, whilst attending the sick and dying, during the terrible famine and epidemics so prevalent in Liverpool during the 1840s.

Having such a large population of poor and destitute inhabitants living in poorly ventilated courts and damp dark cellars, the Scotland Road area was particularly vulnerable to outbreaks of disease. In 1847 a Sanitary Act was passed, the beginning of a gradual process to clear the town of its horrendous slums.

The Health Committee, in an effort to determine the scale of the problem, measured and registered 14,085 inhabited cellars, of which 5,841 contained wells of stagnant water. Notices to quit were served upon 8,878 of the occupants, in up to 200 of the most unhealthy streets of the town.

Five thousand dwellings were cleared entirely and it was stated that prior to the Sanitary Act, 27,128 people inhabited cellars.

The church itself had opened in 1833, after moving from its original site lower down Scotland Road, between Dryden Street and Grenville Street (later Virgil Street).

It was opened as a French Chapel, by Father Jean Gerardot, who had left France in 1793 and, after coming to Liverpool, resided in Mile End. By 1810, a portion of Scotland Road at Mile End was named St Anthony's Place, the continuation north was named New Scotland Road.

A Court in St Anthony's Parish

A view of the squalor in St Anthony's Parish from 1914. This is number 3 Court, Penrhyn Street, with the church looming in the background, behind the court property. Twelve courts existed on this side of the street, and have since been replaced by proper housing.

In 1912 this small area was described as being, '... situated on the north side of Penrhyn Street, containing 116 houses, 113 of which are insanitary. The population is 488, and the death rate per thousand per annum, for the six years 1905 - 1910, is 37.56,'

The following two photographs have an incredible span of 140 years separating them.

This very old photograph is a copy of a Daguerreotype taken in approximately 1845. Kindly loaned to me by Mike Taylor, it features his great, great grandfather, George Taylor, with his wife, Elizabeth. When photographed, he was licensee of the Prince of Wales at 310 Scotland Road (see list, 362). His first pub was the Punch Bowl at 33 Bevington Bush, in the 1830s.

After vacating the Prince of Wales, he became the licensee of the Half Way House for a short spell, before retiring in 1857.

In an 1862 directory he was described as a 'gentleman', residing at 15 Seacombe Street, Everton.

Some 140 years later, in 1984, this photograph was taken, featuring Pat Fitzgerald, the licensee of the Half Way House, and her brother Reg. The pub had been in their family from 1934, when their father, William, was in charge.

After his death in 1940, his wife, Annie, ran the pub until she died in 1956 and Pat took over. Sadly, the family tradition ended in 1984, when the bulldozer moved in.

Half Way House

Formerly listed at 370-374 Scotland Road (earlier at 270) and 2 Bostock Street (listed near number 10 Court as late as the 1960s). This photograph is from 1984, shortly before demolition.

The premises was aptly known locally as Fitzy's, after the Fitzgerald family who managed the pub for half a century. The former Prince of Wales and St Anthony's Church can just be seen to the right of the picture.

The Europa

Located at 376 Scotland Road (earlier at 276) at the other corner of Bostock Street. During the 1860s the pub was called the Cuckoo Vaults and by the 1880s, the Ballarat Vaults (probably rebuilt). The premises took its final name, Europa, in the 1930s. This view, from the early 1990s, features the church of St George, high on the Everton Ridge in the background. The pub stood vacant for some time before demolition in 1999.

Schofield Brothers

Although there are no pubs in Dalrymple Street, this view is of a long-established Mineral Water Manufacturer - Schofields, in existence since the 1870s. The only external difference from this 1904 view is that the tower has been shortened and the chimney demolished. Sadly, for a shocked workforce, the premises closed abruptly on the 20 April 1997. The building has since been destroyed by fire.

Incidentally, this street is named after William Dalrymple, a family friend of a former wine merchant, Richard Andrew Mould, whose name is recorded in the adjoining street; Mould Street.

The Great Eastern

Listed at 416 Scotland Road. Pre-1860s named the Alma Vaults (when numbered 426-430), located at the junction of Dalrymple Street (abolished on its original line). The name on the side window is AM Hollis (the initials standing for Annie May) who was the licensee when photographed in 1908. The same family ran the pub from the 1880s, until approximately the First World War. Listed 1970.

White Swan Hotel

A Beer House pre-1880s, listed at 470-472 Scotland Road and number 1 Nursery Street (abolished). The premises closed in the 1940s and was listed as a Ladies Hairdresser's after the War. This photograph was taken in approximately 1912, when the manager was Augustus Scheller.

The Hamlet

The last pub on the east side of the road, at 484, at the junction of Boundary Street East (originally Croston Street). Listed to John Birchall Cooper, in 1858, and Ann Birchall, Victualler, in 1859. Known as the Star, 1880s, then an unnamed Beer House until just after World War Two, when it became the Hamlet. In this 1908 photograph the manager was John Gerdes. Henry Forsyth, Cart Owner occupied the adjoining premises, currently a Betting Shop.

Local publicans, in the early 20th century had to contend with a branch of the Temperance Society in a former chapel in Boundary Street East: the People's Hall Social Club - Teetotal Crusade. By the 1920s it had become the Bramtoco Social Club.

Others on the east side of Scotland Road were or are:

2	Leeds Arms at number 2, pre-1860s, then the Scotland Hotel, 1870s at 2-4, resuming its earlier title of the Old Leeds Arms 1880s. Not listed 1908 (number 4 also listed as the Wheatsheaf, 1850s).
18	Lamb, pre-1840s. Listed before numerical changes.*
26	Grapes pre-1860s.
28	Hope and Anchor, not listed 1880s.
30	BH and Eating House, by 3 Court. Dining Rooms 1880s.
42	SV, pre-1870s, then the Green Doors, closed c1904, junction of Gay Street (featured as a modern view).
44	SV, junction of Gay Street. Provision Dealer 1880s.
54	BH, pre-1880s.
64	Square and Compass, 1820s. Listed in New Scotland Road before numerical changes.*
64	BH and Smithy, 1840s. Listed before numerical changes.*
72	W & SV listed as Dining Rooms, 1880s.
78	BH and Botanic Beer Maker, 1880s.
88	Bowling Green Inn pre-1840s. Before numerical changes.*
90	White Lion, pre-1840s. Cumberland Arms, 1840s. Listed to Provision Dealer 1860s before numerical changes.*
98	Nelson Tavern pre-1840s, then the Seven Stars up to 1890s, becoming the Wolseley Arms. Not listed 1940s.

Police Report 1898: Selling drink to a drunken man, bound over.

102	SV. Listed as a Confectioner 1860s.
132-134	BH pre-1860, then Clock Vaults. Listed 1964.
138	BH, 1850s.
144	Albion Hotel. Listed as Cocoa Rooms, 1912. Police Report 1900: Permitting drunkenness, dismissed.
152	W & SV pre-1880s, then the Market Inn, junction of McKee Street, closed 1930s.

Police Report 1892: Selling drink to a drunken man, 4/6 + costs.

154a	Brewery pre-1860s, then the Victoria SV, corner of McKee Street (realigned after construction of Victoria Square), listed to a Tea Dealer, 1880s.
162	Golden Fleece until the 1890s, then the Star. Listed to the Empire Clothing Co, 1908, at 160-162.

Police Report 1892: Permitting drunkenness and selling drink to a child under fourteen, dismissed. Notice of objection.

164	Fleece, pre-1860s then the British Workman Public House Co Ltd. Listed as Dining Rooms 1920s.
168	SV 1850s.
172	Summer SV pre-1860s, then a BH. Closed c 1908.

Police Report 1892: Selling drink to a drunken man, 4/6 + costs.

232	SV (1850s, probably part of next pub).
234-236	Old House at Home, listed to a Pawnbroker 1860s.
252	Pineapple pre-1860s, then the Woodman. Closed 1890s.
258	BH 1850s.
260	BH 1850s.
282	SV.
284	Mariners, earlier the Windmill.
296a	SV (by no 15 Court).
312	BH (282-312, mentioned earlier).
354	BH pre-1880s, junction of Newsham Street.
362	Prince of Wales Vaults, at 310 Scotland Road pre-1880s. Became a Furniture Dealer 1904, currently a Butchers.

Police Report 1892: Permitting drunkenness, bound over.

398a	The Great Northern, pre-1880s, then the Northern House at 400, junction of Louis Street. Listed to the Mersey Quay and Railway Carters Union, 1912, at 398-400

Police Report 1892: Selling drink to a drunken man, 10/- + costs.

418	Victoria Vaults pre-1860s (at 432a) then a BH and Botanic Beer Maker. Queen's Arms in the 1890s, closed c 1912, then became a Cabinet Maker's.
426	Gretna Green Inn, earlier at 440, corner of Mould Street, closed c 1908. 1920s Saddlers & Harness Maker's.

Police Report 1900: Permitting drunkenness, dismissed.

448	W & S Dealer and Botanic Beer Maker, closed WW1.
452	BH and Botanic Beer Maker, closed during WW1.
474	BH and Botanic Beer Maker. Dining Rooms 1890s.

* Listed before numerical changes, may have been at a different location.

Like Scotland Road itself, the surrounding district has, over the years, changed beyond all recognition, especially since the 1960s.

The following were all east of Scotland Road.

Some of the following streets are now classed as West Everton, although they are in this section because they were, or are, all in the Liverpool 3 district, which was part of Liverpool when Everton was a separate township (Liverpool 5 and 6).

Cazneau Street, named after Joseph Cazneau, a merchant, who built the first house in the street in the 1790s, has all but vanished since the construction of the second Mersey Tunnel, leading from Scotland Road to St Anne Street pre-1970s. Originally containing 12 pubs, including the following five:

Swan Hotel

A huge corner pub, formerly listed at 12-14 Cazneau Street and 2 Beau Street. No writing is visible on the building, when photographed in the early 1960s.

A once well-known feature of Cazneau Street, in this period, was the lorry, shown on a billboard fronting Scott's Bakery. The lorry has long gone, although the former bakery still remains as a different business. A travelling fair was camped in Beau Street at the time this picture was taken. Listed 1970.

Denbigh Castle

Open to date, as the only pub left on Cazneau Street. It was known locally as Mick Whitty's, after a former manager. When this picture was taken in 1908, it was in the midst of a slum area, with the manager Thomas George Coleman. The address then was 15 Cazneau Street/Number 3 Court (Juvenal Terrace). There is a glimpse of another court to the right of the premises - Peel Square, both now long demolished.

Clock Hotel

Formerly listed at 36 Cazneau Street and 36 Juvenal Street. Known locally as the Birkenhead House, deriving from the brewers, Birkenhead Brewery, when photographed in the early 1960s. Site now part of a widened thoroughfare. Listed 1964.

Prince Arthur Hotel

Situated at 49 Cazneau Street, on the corner of Lawrence Street (abolished), whose former houses are shown. Displaying its name when photographed in 1912, when the manager was John Nixon. Adjoining the pub is the aptly-named Hay Market Café, facing the old Wholesale Fruit, Vegetable and Hay Market. Listed 1964.

Royal Standard Hotel

Located at the junction with Horatio Street (abolished), at number 59 Cazneau Street. Horatio Street and the narrow alley on the right, Boardman Place, both contained court property when photographed in the 1920s. The manager was Owen J Kelly. Listed 1964.

Brewers Arms

Rose Place formerly led from Scotland Road to Fox Street and once contained 14 pubs. It has since been abolished at the Scotland Road end and is now landscaped, with a section remaining containing modern houses. The pub was listed at 18 Rose Place and 35 Comus Street, which once had five pubs and now contains modern housing. The pub probably took its name from the Brewery which once stood on the site. Photograph from the 1920s, when managed by Robert D Taylor and was known as Bob Taylor's until closure. Listed 1970.

Great Richmond Street still remains, from Rose Hill to Fox Street and formerly contained five pubs, including the next two:

Wine & Spirit Vaults

Situated at the junction of Rose Hill and Great Richmond Street, this old establishment closed as long ago as 1903, when its licence expired. Photograph from the 1890s, when managed by John Williams Savage. Pre-1880s named the Liverpool Arms.
Police Report 1892: Permitting drunkenness, dismissed. Also: Domino playing allowed in this house.

Beer House

A typical unnamed Beer House of old Liverpool listed at 49 Great Richmond Street. Listed near number 13 Court when photographed in the 1890s and managed by Mrs Janet Carter, probably the lady in the doorway. Not listed 1908.
Police Report 1892: Domino playing allowed.

During the late 18th and early 19th centuries, St Anne Street was one of the town's most important streets, the name deriving from St Anne's Church (1772). A rapid decline set in during the 19th century, as the slums began to infiltrate the area. Some 23 licensed premises eventually lined the street, including the following three:

The Wellington

Listed at 24 St Anne's Street at the junction of Springfield. The adjoining premises to the right, was also at number 24, as the whole building was originally a Georgian private house. Photographed in 1986 when it was still open, and a fire had just destroyed the adjoining two buildings.

One of these buildings, no 28, a former large warehouse, was a listed building. The other burnt out building on this view has been demolished, whilst the pub has now been closed for a number of years.

This is the Wellington, still standing derelict, when photographed in 2000.

The Grapes

Formerly listed at 31 and 28 Springfield Street (abolished). An old ice-cream cart can be seen in Springfield Street. In the doorway of the pub, three children sit looking down the street - hoping for the ice cream man to return perhaps?

Next to the pub, on St Anne Street, there used to stand a Marble Works, whilst the adjoining house, in Springfield Street, was in use as a Laundry.

Photograph from the 1920s, when managed by Edward Warwick. Listed 1970.

Royal Standard

Located at 64, on the corner of Mansfield Street. Photographed approximately 1970, when the licensee was Mary Harkin. Premises closed and demolished during the 1980s. The site is currently waste ground.

Letters

Off the eastern side of St Anne Street runs the narrow Birkett Street, where this pub, originally one of four, was listed at number 73, where it met a long-demolished alley called Fletcher Gardens. A most inappropriate name, as it contained court property when photographed in the 1890s, the manageress being Martha Walker. Not listed 1908.

The term 'Letters' generally referred to any unnamed public house, although a few pubs, such as this one, were actually so named.

Grapes

Parallel with St Anne Street westward, used to stand Clare Street. This pub was listed at number 33, one of six at the junction of Springfield Street. Both streets were demolished, along with the pub, during the 1970s.

A barefooted boy looks on in this photograph from approximately 1912, when the manager was William Skinley. Premises was renamed the Castle in the 1920s.

West of St Anne Street, Christian Street still remains, now realigned and containing modern housing. One pub remains from a former total of 17, including the following four.

Shakespeare Vaults

Listed at 29-31 Christian Street and 85-87 Gerard Street, this pub was probably named in connection with the nearby theatre. Photographed in the 1920s, when managed by Edwin Pearce. Not listed 1940s.

Also connected with Shakespeare and located at 34, was the Sir John Falstaff, later the Original Falstaff. It may have been destroyed during the War as it was also not listed in the 1940s.

Adelphi Vaults and the Adelphi Theatre

Built as the Olympic Circus Adelphi Theatre in 1795, this view is from the 1890s, when situated at 42-44 (pre-1860s at 34) with the manager Frank Wilson. The premises was also used as a boxing and wrestling venue, then known as the Arena.

In 1912 the theatre was converted to the Adelphi Picture House and in 1921, it was demolished and rebuilt as the New Adelphi Cinema, which was destroyed during World War Two.

Like the Rotunda Vaults, a pub was often attached to the theatre. In this case, it was the Queen's Theatre Tavern, adjacent to the Queens Theatre, also listed at 34, after being renamed, around 1830. The theatre reverted to the Adelphi by 1860, then at 42, and the pub, at 44, was renamed the Adelphi Vaults.

This pub appears to have closed about 1906 and from this date it was listed as a Lodging House. The proprietor of the Lodging House, in 1908, was Joseph Whate, probably the same man, or a relation, who had a Lodging House at the northern end of Scotland Road. Known as Champion Whates, this was a well-known doss house for many years, not just locally, but world wide, frequented particularly by seafarers.
Police Report 1902: Notice of objection.

The Pontack

Open to date, at number 56 Christian Street, on the corner of the former Pontack Lane. One of the oldest and most acclaimed pubs of the street, listed in the 1820s at 44. In the mid 19th century, it was used as an electioneering house during parliamentary and municipal elections and it was the headquarters of the St Anne Ward. The rabid and noisy politicians who fought their party battles in the pub at election times, would often end up keeping the nearby Rose Hill Bridewell well stocked! The pub was also frequented by actors, who, during the last century lodged in houses in the surrounding streets, when performing at the nearby Adelphi Theatre.

The houses adjoining the pub on the left were replaced by modern housing in the 1960s. The manager in the 1920s photograph was Robert Cobbett Yates.

This view, from the 1980s, shows the pub in isolation, with the remnants of Pontack Lane on the right, whilst on the left, is the rear of St Anne's Police Station. Houses have been constructed once again in the vicinity.

Myrtle Vaults

On the corner of Holly Street (abolished) and photographed before the First World War, when managed by Herbert Fleming. Originally named after the street in which it stood, Myrtle Street, renamed in the 1870s to Holly Street. Listed 1970.

One of the former pubs of Christian Street, the Sportsman's Arms (Sol's Arms, pre-1880s) had a Police Report of 1892, part of which could well apply today.

Police Report 1892: The management has not altogether been satisfactory, the house, owing to free and easy concerts, being frequented by young girls and youths in large numbers, who drink and conduct themselves improperly and, for this reason, police consider the retention of the music and singing licence objectionable. Back door of public house and back door of a private house open into enclosed entry, the door of which, if locked, renders police supervision difficult. Also: Permitting drunkenness, dismissed.

Richmond Row led in a north easterly direction from Scotland Place, for some 635 yards, to Everton Brow. Originally, it was the road to Everton and a pleasant country lane in the early 18th century. Like the area in general, it was soon covered by bricks and mortar, becoming a most squalid part of the town.

Since the demolition of the area from the 1960s, west of St Anne Street, there is no trace of Richmond Row, a police station and modern houses cover its site. However, a section to the east of St Anne Street still remains. Twenty-seven pubs and a number of Breweries once lined this thoroughfare, including the following six:

Mason's Arms

Listed at number 22. Very old property on the demolished part of the thoroughfare. Photographed as long ago as 1898, when the manager was Harry Moss Redfearn. To the left of the pub, an entrance to Hamill's Court is featured, with another, Lyon Court to the right. Premises listed to a Cabinet Maker 1912.

Stafford Arms

Listed at number 62. Photographed approximately 1905, when managed by Mrs Mary Stanley. Note the adjoining bread shop, Berry's, advertising 'Hovis Bread as supplied to HM the King', referring to King Edward VII. Not listed 1920s.

St Ann's Hotel

Photograph from 1912, when the manager was Edward Felton Formerly listed at 107-109 Richmond Row and 115 St Anne Street. An open court can be partly seen adjoining the premises on St Anne Street. Listed 1970.
Police Report 1902: Selling drink to a drunken man, bound over.

Richmond Arms

Listed at 163 Richmond Row and 2-4 Fox Street, also photographed 1912 when the manager was William Newall. Premises closed approximately 1928, becoming a Dining Rooms in the 1930s and a Lodging House in the 1940s.

Surprisingly, the structure, although derelict for years, avoided the demolition programme of the area in the 1960s and 70s, only to be demolished in 1995.

Featuring the same view in the early 1990s, having been derelict for years. Note the upper windows, long bricked up. Beyond the block, in Fox Street, is the Church of St Mary of the Angels. Always referred to as the Friary, from the time when Franciscan Monks, in their brown habits, served the local Catholic community and were a familiar site around the neighbourhood.

It was a rare structure indeed to survive, intact, into the 1990s. This block was a three storey, narrow building, having no back windows, as can be seen from this view; once a common feature of buildings in the older parts of Liverpool.

This view of Everton Brow, is taken from Richmond Row in 1999. The vacant land on the left was the site of the Richmond Arms, whilst on the right stands the derelict Soho Public House.

The on-going, city-wide demolition of high-rise flats is shown in the centre. The blocks were named John F Kennedy Heights.

The Clock

Located at 164 Richmond Row, at the junction of Drinkwater Gardens, a very ornate pub, as this pre-First World War photograph shows, when managed by James Watkin Hughes. Pre-1880s, listed as a Beer House and Brewer.

Drinkwater Gardens remains today as an alley, off Richmond Row, although a completely different world from over a century ago, as the following report indicates.

Police Report 1892: This house has, in addition to a large front entrance, no less than four side doors (one of which is a double one), all opening into a narrow entry and court, containing very wretched dwellings.

This modern view is from 1998, having remained vacant for over ten years. It was finally demolished in 1999.

The Loggerheads

Formerly listed at 172-174 (pre-1860s, at 148). One of the oldest pubs on Richmond Row, described as being old as long ago as the 1880s, quite justifiably, as it is shown on a map from 1768. Featuring a large advert for Lewis's Tailoring when photographed pre-First World War and managed by Mrs Harriet Johnson.

The meaning of the word, 'loggerhead', in connection with pubs, no longer in common use, was that of a stupid person. Inns displaying this humorous sign usually had a painting of two silly faces, accompanied by the caption, 'we three loggerheads be'. The unsuspecting reader, making up the third. This particular sign has three faces, so maybe the old joke had worn out!

Somewhat strangely, the pub closed in the early 19th century, to become a private house, and was occupied by a Mr Nicholson, who was Mayor in 1813. Residing constantly with Mr Nicholson's family, was Felicia Browne, later Mrs Hemans, a renowned poetess (1793-1835). Many of her earlier poems were written under this roof. One of her most famous poems was *Casabianca*, containing the immortal line, 'The boy stood on the burning deck'.

After Mr Nicholson vacated the house, it reverted to its previous function and kept the same name. The premises finally closed and was divided up just before the Second World War thus: at number 172 there was a Leather Factory, at 172a, Family Laundry Ltd and at 172b, Tuebrook Bakers.

At the end of Richmond Row/Everton Brow, northward, is Fox Street where the following two, of formerly five pubs were located.

The Fox

Listed at 37 Fox Street, on the corner of Beau Street, is a huge pub, with an even larger warehouse alongside it. The pub closed during the 1930s, and was then listed to a Licensed Broker. Photograph from the 1920s, when the licensee was Hector H Brunst. The adjoining shop in Beau Street (formerly part of the pub) was a Grocer's, listed to William Holmes. The adjoining, warehouse had various uses over the years, including the following during the 1930s: Timpany & Taylor, Washing Machine Manufacturer, Samuel Brown, Artist and the North Western Anglo/Swedish Electrical Welding Co Ltd. The warehouse was not listed in 1940.

The Brown Cow

Situated at 51 Fox Street, at the junction with Juvenal Street. Was the man in the carriage waiting for his picture to be taken when photographed in 1903? The manager at the time was John R Bennett. Listed 1970. (Six pubs were in Juvenal Street)

The pub was known as the Gas House, and was apparently the last Liverpool pub still lit by gaslight during the 1960s. Not too far from here, on Richmond Row, was a pub named the Oil Gas Tavern, which closed in the 1930s.

Southerly from Richmond Row/Everton Brow, is Soho Street, once a heavily-populated street that contained a number of breweries and some 18 pubs. Since the recent reconstruction, Soho Street remains, but not on its original line.

The following five pubs were, or are, on Soho Street:

Volunteer Arms

Listed at 26 at the junction of Roderick Street. Photographed in the late 1960s and demolished in the 1980s.

The Gomer

Listed at 31 Soho Street, on the corner of Gomer Street (abolished). The street formerly contained court property. Closing in the late 1920s, it was then listed to a Confectioner. Pre-1880s it was called the Soho Vaults.

Photograph from the 1920s, when the manager was John Edward Brennan, shows an adjoining Chandler's shop, at 33, belonging to George Flint Howley.

Black Horse Inn

Listed at 61 Soho Street (pre-1860s, at 23) on the corner of Torbock Street (abolished). It closed approximately 1930, as part of a scheme for the construction of municipal walk up flats, which were locally known as the 'Four Squares'. The blocks are now long demolished. Note the bare foot children, next to an elderly person sitting, outside the pub when photographed in 1908. Managed at the time by William Spurgin. The adjoining premises were Cocoa Rooms.

The Soho

Built at 2 Soho Square, this was a Wine & Spirit Vaults pre-1890s and closed approximately 1930. The adjoining section was then listed to a Second Hand Book Seller and, at 2 Soho Square, to a Confectioner. Modern housing now occupies this site. Managed by John Waterson at the time of this 1920s photograph.

The Soho Arms

Listed at 119-121 Soho Street and 182 Richmond Row. Photographed in the 1980s, when still open. Although currently closed, it is the only remaining pub in Soho Street and was known as Broken-Nosed Jack's. Various Breweries were located throughout the 19th and early 20th centuries between numbers 91 and 119. This pub was probably part of a Brewery, as it was not listed separately until approximately 1912, when 107-117 were listed to Lunts Bakery and by the 1960s, 97-117 were listed as United Service Ltd Transport (depot).

The Punch Bowl

This pub could be found at 23 Torbock Street (abolished), off Soho Street. Clearly displaying the name of the manager, T Woloughan, who managed the pub from 1894 - 1901. Pre-1880s listed as a Wine & Spirit Vaults. Listed to a Confectioner in the 1920s.

Police Report 1902: Failing to admit the police to the licensed premises, dismissed. Also: Permitting drunkenness, 10/- and costs.

Two unusually-named pubs of Torbock Street were the Brown Horse and Punch Bowl and the Chestnut Mare, both pre-1860s.

Islington (originally Folly Lane) once had 14 pubs, none of which remains today. The following were four of them.

Kings Arms

Listed at 32 Islington, at the junction of Fraser Street. Photographed in the early 1960s when the manager was Harry E Walker. The site is now part of the area surrounding a bus station. Listed 1970.

The Wellington

A former Mellor's house listed at 33 Islington, at the corner of Christian Street. Photographed in the 1960s when most of the adjoining shops and businesses were becoming vacant, ready for demolition. The manager was Norman H Jones. Listed 1970. The site is now part of a widened thoroughfare.

Police Report 1892: The door of a snug, at the end of the bar, is kept bolted on the inside. The bolting of this door is objectionable, as the police cannot enter the room until the bolt is withdrawn by those in charge of the bar.

Royal Oak

Listed at 44 Islington and 46 Norton Street. The building on the left was also a pub - the Britannia. Photographed in the 1960s, when the manager was James E Clare. Listed 1970. The corner site is currently a car wash.

Birchfield

Listed at 133 Islington, at the junction of Birchfield Street (abolished). The pub and street were named after a former field, through which it was laid out. This field was owned by William Roscoe, who originally had three houses built in the street, prior to the terraced property being erected in the 1850s and 60s.

There is quite a crowd waiting at the bus stop outside the adjoining Richards Cash & Carry Drapers Shop, when photographed in the 1960s, with the pub still open for business. Listed 1970.

Globe Vaults

One of the former streets off Islington, east of Soho Street, was Bidder Street (abolished), where this pub was listed at number 64, one of two pubs on either corner of Langsdale Street.

As illustrated, the street contained landing houses, with the pub standing at the end of the block. The pub's licence expired in 1912. Photographed in the late 1890s, when the licensee was Sarah White. The street was demolished in the 1950s.

The following three pubs, of an original six, were in Canterbury Street, off Islington, now shortened and containing modern housing.

Canterbury Arms

Listed at 25 Canterbury Street and photographed in 1908, when managed by Peter Brownhill. Pre-1880s it was named the Canterbury Hall Vaults and was known locally as the Fish House. Not listed 1940s. A modern pub, the Goblin, was later built on the site.
Police Report 1903: The Bidder Street door opens into a covered passage, 17 yards long, leading to the public house. This passage is very steep, in consequence of Canterbury Street being much higher than Bidder Street, and is difficult of supervision. Also: Selling drink to a drunken man, dismissed.

The Great Eastern

Listed at 57 Canterbury Street and 23 Langsdale Street, taking up the whole block between Canterbury Street and Page Street. A late 19th century public house, typical of the ornate detail that was often put into the design and construction.

This view from the 1980s shows the premises derelict prior to demolition, along with the comparatively modern houses also in the picture, an all-too-familiar occurrence in Liverpool. During the 1990s, houses have once again been built in the vicinity.

Clock Inn

A large public house, located at 104 Canterbury Street and 32 William Henry Street. Photographed in 1912 when managed by Francis H Massey. Modern housing now occupies this spot. Listed 1964.

After the old housing and pub were cleared from the street, a new pub, of the same name, was built in nearby Salisbury Street.
Police Report 1903: Domino playing allowed in this house.

The Bee Hive

Situated in nearby Langsdale Street (originally Church Street, Soho) one of an original four pubs, listed at 39-41, at the junction of Field Street. John Scott was manager from approximately 1912 - 1930s and appears in this 1920s photograph. The pub was still referred to as Scott's until demolition. Listed 1970.
Police Report 1902: Domino playing allowed.

Volunteer Arms

Field Street still remains, containing modern housing, although not on its original line, which was from Everton Brow through to Carver Street, close to Islington. The premises was formerly one of six pubs, listed at 172, at the junction of Barwise Street and had a rear entrance in Back Salisbury Street, now the site of multi-storey flats (due for demolition).

Photographed in 1908 when the licensee was Mary Tarleton, a relative of the renowned boxer, Nel Tarleton, licensee from approximately 1901, until the early 1930s. The faded name, Volunteer Arms, can be seen below the top window and the premises was still locally referred to as Tarleton's until demolition. Nel Tarleton was British Featherweight Champion seven times between 1934 and 1947 and made history by becoming the first man to win two Lonsdale Belts, presented to boxers who successfully defend a British title three times in succession. Listed 1964.

The following two, from an original seven, were in Salisbury Street, off Islington.

Beer House

This old Beer House was listed at 117-119 Salisbury Street, where the road meets Elizabeth Terrace. Although not shown on this view, the pub had an entrance in the terrace, which contained court property.

Photograph from 1908, when the manager was Henry Brayshaw. The pub acquired the name the Salisbury before closure in the 1920s.
Police Report 1903: Card playing allowed in this house.

Windsor Castle

The last of a former five pubs located in William Henry Street, this one is situated at the corner of Page Street. The area surrounding this pub is typical of so many housing schemes built during the 1960s. It was cleared and replaced by housing once again in the 1990s. The pub remained intact throughout these changes, although residents hereabouts would no doubt have been glad to see either the demolition, or renovation, of this vandalised, burnt out former pub, seen here in a state of pitiful disrepair in 1995. It was finally demolished in 2001.

Everton Vaults

Located where Salisbury Street meets Barwise Street, now the site of multi-storey flats (due for demolition). Edward Joseph Gibney managed the pub when photographed during the 1920s. Not listed 1940s. Incidentally, almost facing Barwise Street, stood Coronation Street. Unlike its famous television series namesake, whose setting is in a street of terraced property, court property existed here and the street was only 47 yards in length.
Police Report 1903: Domino and quoit playing allowed in this house.

SFX Football Team

This team belonged to one of the more well-known schools of Liverpool - St Francis Xavier's, or SFX, as it is commonly known, in Salisbury Street. This 1930s photo was supplied by Tony Jordan, whose father, Luke, was one of the team.

The St Francis Xavier's Society was established in 1840 for the purpose of building a church and college. The church was consecrated in 1848 and five years later the construction of the schools commenced. The foundation stone was laid by Alderman Richard Sheil on the 15 August 1853, opening October 1854. After the blessing, the Right Reverend Bishop Brown presented a silver trowel to Mr Sheil, which bore the following inscription:

'Presented to Richard Sheil Esq, on the occasion of the laying of the foundation stone of the poor schools of St Francis, Liverpool, the Feast of the Assumption.'

On the reverse side was an engraved sketch of the intended schools.

Richard Sheil was a popular figure of his time in Liverpool and in the days of entrenched bigotry, was the only Roman Catholic on the Town Council. Sheil Road and Sheil Park, Liverpool 6, were named in honour of him.

His eldest son married a Miss Leonard, who resided in a large house in Everton Valley. Her home was later converted to a convent, occupied by the nuns of Notre Dame, still in use to date as Notre Dame School. During the mass demolition of the vicinity in the 1960s, Notre Dame High School actually took in a number of girls from St Francis Xavier's.

Other children were dispersed to various schools, with some of the boys going to Campion High School, Prince Edwin Street and others to the Friary, Bute Street.

St Francis Xavier's College, attended by pupils who had passed the eleven plus, moved out to Beaconsfield Road, Woolton, about 1960, remaining there to date.

The site around the church is currently undergoing a massive regeneration programme, to become part of the Hope College.

Prior to the mass demolition of the area, St Francis Xavier's was once the largest Catholic parish in the country.

Leaving the eastern vicinity of Scotland Road and moving to the western area, we arrive at the most deprived and over-crowded part of Liverpool during the 19th century, illustrated by the following map of 1875. Note the death rate in Sawney Pope Street compared to Rodney Street. Incidentally, Sawney Pope Street changed names to Alexander Pope Street in the 1890s.

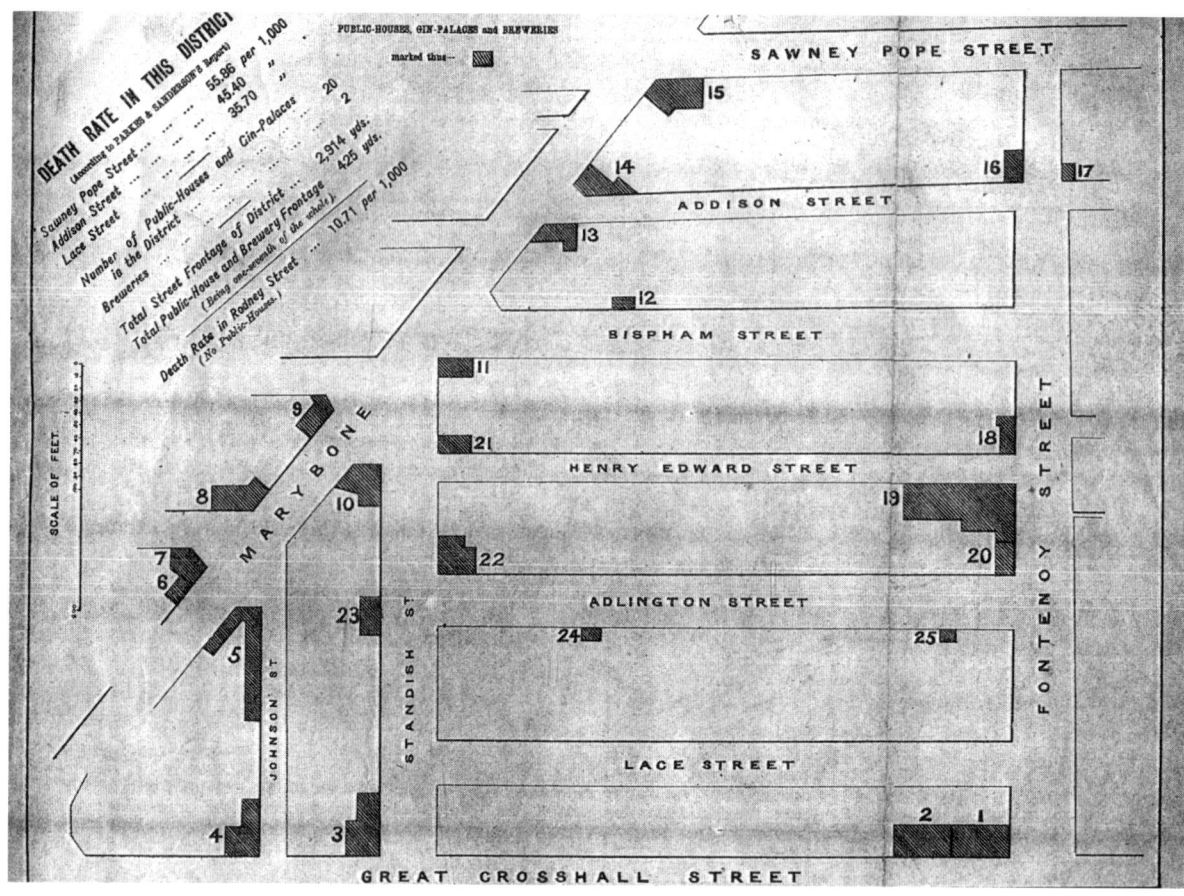

DEATH RATE IN THIS DISTRICT
(According to PARKES & SANDERSON'S Report)
Sawney Pope Street ... 55.86 per 1,000
Addison Street ... 45.40 "
Lace Street ... 35.70 "
Number of Public-Houses and Gin-Palaces ... 20
Breweries ... 2
Total Street Frontage of District ... 2,314 yds.
Total Public-House and Brewery Frontage ... 425 yds.
(Being one-seventh of the whole.)
Death Rate in Rodney Street ... 10.71 per 1,000
(No Public-Houses.)

PUBLIC-HOUSES, GIN-PALACES and BREWERIES marked thus—

The premises and managers on this map were as follows:

1. 67-69 Gt Crosshall Street
   Australian Vaults
   Hugh Flanagan
2. 63 Gt Crosshall Street
   Liverpool Arms
   John McCormick
3. 19 Gt Crosshall Street
   Borough Vaults
   Thomas Richardson
4. 9 Gt Crosshall Street
   Mountain Dew
   John Hopwood
5. 8-12 Marybone
   Copeland & Green
   Janet Beattie
   Marybone Brewery
6. 39 Marybone
   Prince Albert
   Janet Beattie
7. 41 Marybone
   Spirit Vaults
   Elizabeth White
8. 43 Marybone
   Wrekin
   William Kirkbride
9. 51-53 Marybone
   Marlborough Hotel
   William Patterson
10. 24 Marybone
    Wine & Spirit Vaults
    Joseph Clegg
11. 2 Bispham Street
    Wine & Spirit Vaults
    Elizabeth Lee
12. 11 Bispham Street
    Beer House
    Andrew Cummings
13. 30 Marybone
    Great Western
    James Savage
14. 32 Marybone
    Justice Hotel
    David Davis
15. 42 Marybone
    Grapes
    John McCandlish
16. 97 Fontenoy Street
    Grapes
    Charles Skuse
17. 98 Fontenoy Street
    Wine & Spirit Vaults
    Ann Clark
18. 79 Fontenoy Street
    Railway Vaults
    Thomas Nolan
19. 75-77 Fontenoy Street
    Brewery Public House
    J Glover & Sons (Brewers)
20. 69-75 Fontenoy Street
    Wine & Spirit Vaults
    & Public House
    J Glover & Sons (Brewers)
21. 52 Standish Street
    Beer House
    Margaret Weedon
22. 46 Standish Street
    Adlington Arms
    Henry Irwin
23. 39 Standish Street
    Old House at Home
    George Brown
24. 16 Adlington Street
    Beer House
    Isabella Yeoman
25. 52 Adlington Street
    Swan Vaults
    William Maudle

Although the map states that the district was the most unhealthy in the city, in reality, similar conditions existed on a much wider scale, including the entire Exchange, Vauxhall and Scotland Wards, during the Victorian years. Also, the map, like some of the old lists, does not include all the pubs that once existed in the area and also omits the insanitary courts, so abundant in this locality. The following is one such court.

The following were all west of Scotland Road.

This entrance is to number 10 Court, whose exact whereabouts is unknown, although it was located within the area covered by the map. The squalid conditions in this type of court are difficult to believe nowadays. Once through the first narrow passage, other narrow passages led off in various directions, to atrocious housing, where light and fresh air were unknown commodities. Sanitation was at its most crude in these hovels and it is no surprise that disease and death were everyday occurrences.

The terrible conditions of the earlier courts were gradually improved through various acts of the 19th century. With an ever-increasing population, and so many insanitary courts and cellars, it was an uphill task. One of the schemes to improve the situation involved the removal of the front of houses, so creating an open court. Although not a cure, this measure did enable a certain amount of fresh air and light to penetrate the dwellings. Of greater benefit, was the installation of ashbins, a system brought into use by 1898.

By the time of the First World War, just over 400 courts existed throughout Liverpool (1,510 stood in 1895). Despite the authorities' efforts to clear them, cellars classed as unfit for humans were still inhabited and it would be many years before such property was eradicated. The 1960s was the decade in which courts were finally cleared.

Cellars were supposed to be uninhabited by 1912, as the following report states:

'Under the provisions of the Liverpool Corporation (General Powers) Act, 1908, the occupation of cellars, as separate dwellings, the floors of which are more than two feet below the ground, must cease after 31 December 1912.'

The number of inhabited cellars in 1912 was about 1,600, (about half the number from ten years previously), containing a population of about 5,000, whose chief occupations were described as: dock and casual labourers, marine firemen, carters and charwomen.

The figure for 1912, although still outrageous, was a massive improvement from the mid 19th century. The atrocious living conditions for people living in cellars had been recognised during the 1840s. The repugnant dwellings had in fact started to be cleared in the late 1840s: it was recorded that 3,000 cellars had been closed in 1849, still leaving 11,000 occupied by some 27,000 people.

The location of cellar dwellings in 1912 was as follows:

District	Number of cellar dwellings
Scotland	552
Exchange	46
Abercromby	56
Everton	503
Kirkdale	105
West Derby (West)	83
Toxteth	268

The deplorable conditions of the poor can best be illustrated by the infant mortality rate during the late Victorian years. In England, the rate was 142 per 1000 births and, whilst Liverpool, in general, was 183, Vauxhall Ward was 264. The general rate of infant mortality in Liverpool, by 1912, had dropped to 125 per 1000.

Medical opinion attributed the high death rate in Vauxhall to overcrowding, poor housing and ventilation, inadequate clothing, errors in feeding and violence due to parents' drunkenness.

The following is an extract from a letter written by the Rev RH Lundie in 1880, concerning 'Housing and Public Houses':

'We confined ourselves to two streets and the courts entering from them. In every house there was the appearance of gnawing poverty. In two or three, a faint effort seemed to be made to keep up some show of decent cleanliness; but in the rest ,there was squalor and degradation. In some cases, large families, or numerous persons aggregated otherwise by the family tie, dwelt together in small court houses, for which they paid two shillings or two and six a week. The furniture was the meanest. A small round, deal table was to be seen in most rooms and one, two, or more chairs, or portions of chairs, with sometimes, a little settle, used as a bed at night; and, failing chairs, an old wooden box or two for seats. It was frequently difficult to find any place on which to sit down; the state of the furniture was often offensive enough. It need scarcely be added that the garments of the inhabitants corresponded in cleanliness and cohesion with the furniture. Some of the people go more or less to a mission hall, but none of them, except one Roman Catholic, appeared to have any recognisable connection with any church or chapel. One ragged, weeping woman, in answer to the enquiry, how was her husband employed, told us that he was in hospital with typhus fever. Several others informed us that their children had been suffering from low fever, and that thus, their distress and poverty were aggravated. To breathe the atmosphere of these filthy dens for a few minutes, was all too suggestive of fever. Tattered, ill-fed, bright-eyed children, of whose future we thought with a shudder, were hovering around an almost fireless grate, or rushing in and out from the filthy street, to the filthier home.

Such moral wastes remain as deserts, as if no social or temperance reform were in progress. We may be removing, here and there, an imperilled child to a purer home in Canada but, on the desolate region itself, we have not wrought the slightest change. We have not even touched its fringe. Poverty-stricken it remains in the midst of wealth; criminal in the midst of both law and gospel; dirty, drunken, dissolute, diseased, in the midst of civilisation and Christianity.

It is a matter of course that the police have no employment here. We passed the house of one young woman, perhaps two or three summers over twenty, who, as I was told, had been fifty times in gaol; her return was to this waste.

A visit to Mr Clarke Aspinall's Court of the drunken, on a Monday morning, would show its proportion of tattered and filthy men and women from this region.

A little talk with the inhabitants, leaves no doubt that, in their opinion, their condition has, in most cases, a very close connection with the "house at the corner". As we left the leading street and into the district by a narrow lane, we passed a thriving public house at one corner and a busy pawnbroker's shop at the other. As we left the district, with its many hundreds of blighted families, public houses greeted us again.'

Another everyday occurrence in squalid Liverpool, not referred to in the previous report, but well-documented in others, was wife beating. This was an accepted ordeal for women, particularly on Saturday nights, when few of them would avoid a beating from their drunken husbands. Together with drunken brawls and other evils connected with vile living conditions, to the rest of society, they were simply, out of sight out of mind. But was such behaviour confined to the so-called lower classes? Was wife beating normal across all boundaries of society?

It would appear so, at least in the 17th century, from the following extract taken from a book written in 1795, concerning an epitaph on the depository of Thomas Atherstone, in St Nicholas' Church, who was, according to the town records, bailiff, together with Richard Bushell in 1668. It would seem to be that he was an exception to wife beating, as the following extract states:

'This inscription is a valuable piece of antiquity rescued from oblivion, there is perhaps no other church in England which can boast the remains of a man, so divinely good, that none of his neighbours could ever discover it, or that brought evidence of his peaceable disposition towards the rest of mankind, because he never beat his wife.'

The deplorable conditions endured by the poor of Victorian Liverpool were gradually improved as the 20th Century progressed. The following extracts, concerning the Right Hon John Burns, President, Local Government Board, are from 1910.

'On the previous night, unknown to anybody, between seven and half past ten o'clock, he revisited Dryden Street, Comus Street, Gerard Street, Penrhyn Street, Baptist Street, Juvenal Street, Homer Street, Ben Jonson Street, Milton Street and all the streets with grand titles, but not handsome environments.'

He was proud and pleased to tell his Liverpool contemporaries that, over thirty years, 'there was a revolution in what he saw: over twenty years, a great change and, over ten years, solid, substantial progress, of which Liverpool's poor particularly had every reason to be proud and pleased.'

He rejoiced as he walked down Gerard Street and saw the bricked up cellars which, thirty years ago, were hives of human misery.

Liverpool, to its eternal credit, had got rid of four hundred drinking shops in ten years and over seven hundred in twenty years.

The following quote is an extract from a speech by Mr Burns:

'I want to talk, if I may, to the people who live at Sefton Park and Wavertree and also to those who live across the river, who are in Liverpool, when it suits them, and out of it when it pleases them.

In Sefton Park, where the comfortable classes live, six per ten thousand die annually of tuberculosis, while in Exchange Division, thirty-one per ten thousand die, a mortality which is five times as great. To those people in Sefton Park I say, the measure of your immunity from this scourge ought to be the standard of your benevolent help to the poor people.

I come now to the general death rate. In Wavertree, the general death rate is ten per thousand and in Exchange thirty-one per thousand, which is three times as great.

Then, as to infant mortality, listen to this, ladies of Tranmere, Sefton Park, Wavertree and elsewhere. In Wavertree only eighty-five per thousand of the children born, die within the twelve months. In Exchange, two hundred and fifty-five per thousand die, or three times as many.'

All the following were, or are, in Liverpool 3, with some exceptions as stated. Great Crosshall Street is still a main thoroughfare and although not one of its pubs remains, it once had seventeen, including the following four.

Borough Hotel

Listed at 19 Great Crosshall Street and 17 Standish Street. Photographed in the 1980s, when still open for business, this former Threlfall's pub closed in 1991. The premises has since been converted into accommodation for students. Pre-1890s it was named the Borough Vaults, and in the 1860s, the Commercial Hotel.

Australian Vaults

Formerly listed at 67-69 Great Crosshall Street and 51 Fontenoy Street. This photograph was taken when the pub was closed in the 1980s. It has since been demolished and the site is currently a small car park.

The Dart

Listed at 84 Great Crosshall Street and 52 Fontenoy Street. Only so named since just after the Second World War, previously listed as a Beer House (not on map). In an effort to continue trading, the premises was renamed Patrick's Bar in 1992. However, with the general decline of local pubs and falling population in the area, it closed in 1993 and has since been converted into living accommodation. The demolition of Gerard Gardens is in progress in the background when photographed in the late 1980s.
Police Report 1903: Permitting drunkenness, dismissed.

Old Porter Butt

Listed at 94 Great Crosshall Street, formerly near Byrom Street (not on map). This old pub's licence expired in 1914. Photograph from the 1890s when the manager was John Shaw.

The two shops either side were: at 92, Lewis Williams, the Herbal Beverage Co and at 94a, Herbert Titchmarsh - Tallow Chandler, which became incorporated into the pub.

Six pubs were originally on the south side of Great Crosshall Street (none on map). One of them, the Dublin Castle, was the subject of a police report:

Police Report from 1892: There is a small wicket in one of the back doors and, although the door does not appear to be used, the presence of the wicket might be an encouragement to illicit trading. (In plain English, a stay behind pub!)

Viewing Marybone (originally Bevington Bush Road) today, with its neat new houses and single pub, it is difficult to imagine that it once contained some 27 pubs, including the following.

Wine & Spirit Vaults

Listed at number one Bevington Bush Road, pre-1880s it was called the Hand and Heart (not on map). Photographed in the 1890s, when the manager was James Cunningham. Advertised in the window is Dunville's old Irish whiskey, with 'VR' in between (Victoria Regina). Not listed 1912.

The adjoining shop was the Exchange Printing & Type Writing Co (Printers).

Police Report 1898: Selling drink to a drunken man, bound over.

The Justice Hotel

Found on the corner of Addison Street at number 32. This view is from the 1920s, when the manager was John Joseph McEvoy. Marybone is to the left of the photograph. Listed 1970.

Prince Albert

Formerly listed at 39 Marybone, at the junction with Pickop Street and, pre-1870s named the Marybone Castle. Photograph from 1908, when managed by Hugh Hamill. Adjoining this pub, at number 41, stood a Spirit Vaults which was managed by John Strickland. The two pubs amalgamated in approximately 1909 and closed, due to a compulsory purchase order, in 1926.

Police Report 1903: Renewal objected to on personal grounds, but the then licensee being ill, was granted, on the understanding that the case should be mentioned again. The licence has been transferred and there is now no objection.

Marlborough Hotel, Spirit Vaults and Wrekin

This photograph shows three public houses on one block, between Pickop Street and Marlborough Street: the Wrekin on the far left, at number 43, where a lamp can be seen on the premises, a Spirit Vaults at 45, adjoining (not on map) and, at the forefront, at the junction of Marlborough Street, is the Marlborough Hotel, at 51-53.

Both 43 and 45 closed about the time of the First World War but, somehow, the Marlborough Hotel avoided the bulldozer and war damage and still stands to date.

Finally named the Marlborough Arms Hotel. This photograph was taken in the 1980s when derelict and partially demolished. However, the premises has since reopened as a public house, named Monro's, although it is currently closed.

Organ Vaults

Listed at 123 Marybone on the corner of Naylor Street and photographed in the 1920s, when managed by James Walsh. A small motif above the door reads; William Cole, 4 Clayton Square. A William Cole was listed at this address in 1905 as a Painter. Presumably he painted the Walker's sign, horse and decoration shown on this view.

It changed its name to the Lighthouse during the 1930s and was destroyed by fire in approximately 1950 (not on map).
Police Report 1903: Permitting drunkenness, dismissed.

It is commonly asserted that the youth of today are rowdy, good-for-nothing hooligans, particularly by the older generation. While this is true of a minority of young people, of course, in reality, there has always been a delinquent element, whatever the era. The Teddy Boys of the 1950s, for example, were frowned upon by older people. The High Rip Gang may sound as if they belonged to the 1950s yet, as the following report from 1887, concerning Marybone explains, they were operating way back in the 1880s.

'Marybone begins at the top of Great Crosshall Street and runs northwards to Midgehall Street, Sawney Pope Street and Banastre Street being perhaps the three most famous tributaries which flow from the main line of Marybone. All these streets have, I believe, figured pretty prominently in the police courts and are not altogether unknown in the annals of crime and murder.

The well-lighted public houses which brighten up the corners of these decaying thoroughfares are the only places in this slough of despond which make any approach to comfort, and small blame can attach to the man or woman who is tempted to escape from the atmosphere of foul-smelling paraffin lamps, cold, flagged cellars, knock-down kennels of houses and to forget the squalor and discomfort of home in the poor man's club at the corner. It is indeed rather a matter of wonder, that the revolt against the laws of society, which have forced these people to live as they are doing, has not taken some shape even more dangerous than intemperance and Saturday night rows, relieved in their monotony by the occasional stabbing, or kicking to death, just to give a flavour and spice to the dullness of existence, under such dismal circumstances.

To the bulk of people, Marybone and its perils are an unknown land - associated in their minds with High Rippery and poverty. Marybone, however, is only on the frontier of High Rip land, which really lies further north. I should say that basket women and the lower class of hawkers affect this neighbourhood most. At the same time, I should be sorry to say that the High Rippers do not occasionally sweep down upon the neighbourhood like the hordes of Timur, the Tartar conqueror.

I met a couple of policemen who had just performed the dangerous duty of dispersing a crowd of eighteen or twenty blackguards, who had been carrying on their drunken revels rather too boisterously, either for the peace of the neighbourhood, or the safety of the alarmed publican, of whose premises they had taken possession.

I could not help being struck with the dangers which the police must encounter in the neighbourhood of Marybone, although the risks there are much smaller than in the more northern district of Scotland Road.

I asked one of the officers if he was a believer in the High Rip Gang, as an organised body, and he told me that he did not believe at all, in any organisation of the sort. "There are," said he, "always a large body of men in this neighbourhood, who have no regular work, who in fact, seem to do no work, and how then, do they exist? I have to work for my living, and you for yours, but these men don't, is it any wonder then, that they are up to mischief? They lounge about in little crowds at the corner of streets, and are only too glad of an opportunity of laying their hands on anyone who may afford the chance of plunder. They are mostly growing boys, from thirteen and fourteen years of age upwards. Of course, the danger is not the fear of two or three of them, but of the crowds of them who hang about the district."

While conversing with the policeman, I experienced a feeling of gratitude, that I did not belong to the force. Let any reasonable man visit this neighbourhood and ask himself if he would not demand some more effective arms than a mere truncheon.'

Elderly people also frequently claim that crimes of violence and burglary were rarely heard of in the old days. The following is a list of crimes in Liverpool from 1913.

Indictable offences

Offences against the person	396
Offences against property with violence	1749
Offences against property without violence	8925
Malicious injuries to property	22
Forgery and offences against the currency	57
Other offences	166

Non indictable offences

Assaults, including assaults against the police	2573
Unlawful possession of goods	285
Frequenting with intent to commit felony	220
Malicious damage to property	166
Brothel-keeping	111
Soliciting prostitution	1124
Drunkenness	13347
Cruelty to children	159
Cruelty to animals	312
Begging and sleeping out	958
Gaming etc (Vagrancy Act)	895
Sanitary laws	1759
Offences by owners and drivers of carts	420
Stage carriage and Hackney carriage regulations	51
Street obstructions and nuisances	380
Local acts and bye laws	7204
Elementary education acts	1477
Other offences	2775

Various outcomes from the proceedings occurred: convictions, discharges, probation, abscondings, etc. Forty-one were found to be insane and 137 people were ordered to be delivered to naval or military authorities, a punishment unknown nowadays. Another notorious form of punishment, not in use today, was the birch.

The following is from the same year and concerns offences committed by children, aged 10 to 16 years.

Forgery	1
Breaking and entering	215
Embezzlement	15
Simple larceny	1323
Vagrancy (begging, sleeping out etc)	312
Indecency	6
Other offences	243

Of the total number of offences (2115), 1565 were brought before the courts and dealt with as follows.

Committed to reformatories	118
Committed to industrial schools	113
Whipped with birch rod	285
Bound over	157
Parents ordered to give security	8
Parents ordered to pay compensation	1
Discharged	808
Fined	54
On remand	27

The figure of 285 children birched, would seem totally barbaric to some people, whilst others would have the birch back today. The argument over its use has continued since abolition and will probably continue for some time yet, although, with the arrival of the new millennium and the punishment fading from living memory, the dwindling band of people in favour of its return, will almost certainly never see it.

Crime has always been in our midst and, looking back even further, to when punishments were really cruel and offenders were hanged, drawn and quartered, burnt alive, tortured etc, crimes were still committed.

One recorded incident during the 18th century was the punishment received by a soldier in 1745. After returning from leave, a few hours late, he was treated as a deserter, and was given 700 lashes – a common practice of the time. Even after certain death, the corpse would continue to be lashed until the punishment was complete.

Fontenoy Street, like Marybone, now contains neat, modern housing, a far cry from its former status, when it contained seventeen pubs, including the following two. Incidentally, this is the only street in Liverpool whose name commemorates a British defeat - the Battle of Fontenoy 1745.

Wine & Spirit Vaults

Located at number 98 Fontenoy Street at the junction of Addison Street, stood another old unnamed pub. Closing approximately 1908, it was later listed to a shopkeeper. Addison Street today contains modern housing. Photograph from the 1890s when the manager was William Atkinson.

The Red Lion

Formerly located at the junction of Fontenoy Street and Dale Street and called the Plumber's Arms pre-1880s. The narrow entrance adjacent to the pub was one of two that led into Darwin Court (the other was in Dale Street).

The premises closed in the 1930s and the site's immediate vicinity was built on as Blackburn Chambers, still remaining. Robert Morris was born in this court in 1735. Emigrating to America, he became one of the most successful financiers of his time. In 1776 he was a signatory of the American Declaration of Independence. He was also the founder of the Bank of North America, America's first national bank. After speculating in land deals, he became bankrupt and ended up in a debtors' prison in Philadelphia. Sadly it was here that he died, in 1806, as he was born - in poverty.

One of the former pubs of Fontenoy Street was at number 79, on the corner of Henry Edward Street. Pre-1890s it was called the Railway Vaults and then named the Why Not.

This name became popular from the 1890s, after a famous racehorse - Why Not, which won the Grand National in 1894. A pub of the same name, open to date, in Harrington Street, in the city centre, displays a picture of the horse outside the premises.

The following two, from an original 13, were in Standish Street.

Adlington Arms

At the junction of Adlington Street and Standish Street at 44-46. Photograph from the 1890s, when the manager was John Richards. Pre-1880 it was called the Old House at Home. Listed 1970.

The Wedding House
Formerly situated at 52 Standish Street, at the corner of Henry Edward Street. Named as a Beer House on the map. Not listed 1912.

Beer House

Formerly listed at 16 Adlington Street, one of four pubs right in the midst of the area covered by the previous map and typical of the district. A court entrance (number twenty) is clearly shown adjoining the pub. Photographed in the 1890s, when the licensee was Bridget Gallagher. The premises was named the Irishman's House prior to closure. Not listed 1908.

Wine & Spirit Vaults

Listed at 2 Bispham Street, at the junction of Standish Street. Photograph from 1908 when the manager was James Fitzgerald and featuring a narrow court entrance in Bispham Street and an open court entrance in Standish Street. The street names are displayed on the glass of the gas lamp. Premises not listed 1930s.
Police Report 1892: Selling drink during prohibited hours, dismissed. Back door opens into an entry which leads into a court and police supervision difficult.

Limekiln Lane (originally Back Lane) used to lead from Bevington Bush, northward, as far as Silvester Street. Since the construction of Kingsway (second Mersey Tunnel) it has been physically cut, with a walkway now crossing the tunnel entrance. Numbers 1-79 and 2-64 were, or are, in Liverpool 3, the remainder in Liverpool 5.

Limekiln Lane once contained twenty-three pubs, including the following three, each of which has now disappeared.

Bevington Bush Hotel

Listed at number 2 Limekiln Lane and 1 Bevington Hill, during the early years of the 19th century it was called the Bush Inn a name which was probably of very early origin. By the 1860s it was named the Old Bush Inn Revived, indicating that it would have been rebuilt in that period.

The pub's nickname, the Bevvy, is said to be where the slang word, bevvy, meaning drink, comes from, whilst the name 'Bush' derives from the Shakespearian maxim, 'good wine needs no bush,' reminiscent of the Middle Ages when a bush was a common inn sign.

Photograph from 1912 when the manager was Maurice Cook. Listed 1964.
Police Report 1903: Licensed for music and dancing.

The church in Bevington Hill was St Bridget's, originally a Methodist Chapel, which reopened in 1870 and was sadly largely destroyed during the War. During the 1870s, a number of courts and a public house named the George and Dragon were demolished for the construction of the school shown in Limekiln Lane.

The name Bevington Bush and that of a former nearby inn, the Summer Seat House, conjure up an image of rural tranquillity. Both inns were surrounded by pleasant gardens in the midst of open fields and rural lanes in the early 19th century.

In the days of slave trading and privateering, men dealing in such trades, when returning to Liverpool and having been paid off, would make their way to the inns in question, probably after firstly frequenting dock side pubs, as the following extract from 1887 explains:

'Many a bout of drinking no doubt these cottages have seen when a rich prize has been brought into the river, her decks may be wet with the blood of those who vainly sought to save her from capture and paid the forfeit with their lives. The slavers, crews and privateersmen, flushed with drink and prize money, would echo the sound of noisy revelry across the quiet fields, and along the leafy lanes, through which the boisterous company would ultimately make their way back to Liverpool and their ships.'

When this was written in the 1880s, the days of slave trading and privateering were long finished and the majority of the impoverished inhabitants of the vicinity would probably never have heard of them. Likewise, the rural scenario of some 70 years earlier would have been difficult to imagine. The area at that time had long been slum-ridden, as the following extract, also from 1887, indicates:

'Bevington Bush, as it is situated in the heart of squalid Liverpool, the district in which the officials of the insanitary property committee find the greatest scope for their activity.'

The old inns themselves, like the former rustic surroundings, were also long gone by this time. The Bush had been replaced by the pub in this view, whilst the old Summer Seat House had been replaced by a monster gin palace called the White Lion.

Mill Vaults

Listed at 119 Limekiln Lane and 1 Myers Place, pre-1890s it was called the Miller's Arms. Photograph from 1908, when the manager was William Prior.

In the 1890s the premises facing this pub had been converted to the Food and Betterment Association; a charitable organisation run by a well-known benefactor of Liverpool's poor, Herbert Lee Jackson Jones. Later known as the League of Welldoers and still operational today as the Lee Jones Centre.

Myers Place (abolished) was a small street close to Hornby Street. The Mill Vaults was compulsorily purchased approximately 1930.

Grapes Hotel

This former Threlfall's pub was listed at 100 Limekiln Lane and 201-203 Hornby Street (pre-1860s at 97, when listed next to 39 Court, and named Jones Spirit Vaults). The manager during the 1950s, when photographed was Harry Holmes and the pub was known by his name. A section of the former landing houses on Hornby Street can also be seen. They replaced the enormous number of courts of Hornby Street, some 52 in total. Listed 1970.

The Following five pubs, from a former total of 14, were on Bevington Hill.

The Wellington

Listed at number 2 Bevington Hill. A typical view of the Scotland Road vicinity around 1970, when the area was undergoing mass demolition. The pub featured, at the junction of Wellington Street and Bevington Hill, miraculously survived, only to close and undergo demolition in the late 1980s.

The building on the right was formerly Arden House, since demolished. Built as the Bevington Bush Hotel (Hostel) replacing an old Brewery named the Bevington Bush Brewery.
Police Report 1902: Selling drink to a drunken woman, dismissed.

Maid of Erin

Situated at number 10 Bevington Hill, on the corner of Ellenborough Street, pre-1880s named the Nightingale. This street led from Bevington Hill, to Scotland Road and its site is now part of the Mersey Tunnel entrance.

This photograph shows the pub in 1908, when the manager was James Mason. An entrance to former court property is shown adjoining the premises. Prior to demolition, it was known locally as Hogan's. Listed 1970.

Market Inn

Listed at 16-18 Bevington Hill, at the junction of Maddox Street. An Ind Coope house and managed by Margaret Murtagh when photographed in the 1950s. Listed 1970.

Aptly-named, as the huge pillars shown adjoining the pub constituted the entrance to St Martin's Market. This opened in 1826, on the site of an old quarry and rapidly obtained the nickname, Paddy's Market, (currently in Great Homer Street). The market was largely destroyed during the War, although trading did continue in the open for some time afterwards. The pillars, locally nicknamed the Woodbines, were still standing until well after closure. Although still in living memory, this was not the only Paddy's Market. One was located in the former slum-ridden Banastre Street, between Vauxhall Road and Marybone. Officially named St Patrick's Bazaar (hence the nickname) although in a different world from today, as the following extract from 1883 indicates:

'At the top of Banastre Street, a spectacle is to be witnessed, which cannot be seen anywhere else in Liverpool. It is a striking example of trade in its most rudimentary form. Here is held what is known as Paddy's Market. Inside this place, about three o'clock in the afternoon, you may see a most extraordinary gathering of tattered humanity. The place is densely crowded by a shouting, gesticulating, swearing and generally animated mob. Buyers and sellers were nearly all women, and the articles bought and sold appeared to be mostly rags.'

A variety of eating outlets, ranging from Cocoa Rooms to Dining Rooms, Refreshment Houses, Eating Houses and the Bristish Workman Public House Company, were also once very common in the Scotland Road area. A well-known and very popular one was known as Scouse Alley, located in St Martin's Hall (Paddy's Market).

A similar establishment was located in the nearby Wellington Street, named the Scouse Boat, where many a halfpenny plate of stew was dispensed to eager hungry mouths.

Butcher Boy Vaults

This unusually-named pub was photographed in 1905 when the manager was Adam Montgomery. It was listed at number 49 Bevington Hill and closed in the 1920s. In the window are posters advertising Barnum and Bailey's Circus, to be held at Newsham Park. A nearby pub, at 41, was named the Butcher's Arms.

The Star

Listed at number 85 Bevington Hill and 210 Burlington Street, (pre-1880s at 67, when at the junction of Back Burlington Street). Photograph from the 1960s, when the manager was Thomas Henry. The large adjoining structure was listed to Liverpool Education Committee, Children's Dining Centre and Dental Clinic. Built in 1904, as the Medical Mission Hall, the pub would probably have been rebuilt at about that time. Listed 1970.

The following four pubs were in Burlington Street at the northern limit of Liverpool 3. This street once contained approximately 44 courts, and some 30 pubs.

Beer House

A typical cellar-type property at 129 Burlington Street, displaying a large sign, advertising a price of 2d a pint. Photographed in 1908, when the manageress was Mrs Ellen Donnolly. Named the Durham Ox before closure. Not listed 1912.

Engineer's Vaults

Listed at 142 Burlington Street. Its name, although faded, is shown on the facade when photographed in 1905, then managed by Isaac Davies. It boasted quite a few adverts including 2d a pint for mild ale and bitter and mild at 2½d, a pint.

Also advertised - Persses Galway Whiskey, John Jamison Old Irish Whiskey, Drogheda Stout and McKeown's Pale India Ale. A small advert for Threlfalls, can be seen, although the registered owner was named as Gardner, Thomson & Cardwell, of Whittle Springs Brewery, Chorley. The premises closed around 1908 and became a Boot Repairer's.

Queen Mab

A former Wine & Spirit Vaults listed at 164 Burlington Street and 62 Limekiln Lane. Few customers would have realised that Queen Mab was the fairy queen of old English folklore. A statue adorns the pub - that of Queen Mab perhaps?

Note the barefoot child amongst the onlookers when photographed approximately 1908. The tall man in the doorway, wearing the blocker, (docker's slang for a bowler hat) is probably the manager, Nelson Murray, and the man next to him is wearing a more conventional cap and attire of the working class of the period. Premises was occupied by a Fried Fish Dealer, 1930s.

The Golden Fleece

Pre-1880s the pub was called Thompson's Spirit Vaults. Listed at 171 Burlington Street, at the corner of Titchfield Street. Were these three men waiting for opening time in this 1920s photograph? It was managed by Joseph Walsh until it closed in the late 1920s and was then taken over by a butcher. Modern housing now occupies the site.

The remaining pubs in this section were in Liverpool 5.

Tatlock Vaults

A rather bare-looking corner local, formerly listed at 93 Titchfield Street and 33 Tatlock Street, photographed in the 1950s, when the manager was Arthur P Williams. The pub was known affectionately as Effin' Nellie's for many years, after a character who, as her nickname suggests, was prone to swearing! Listed 1970.

The Grapes

Located at 33-35 Blenheim Street, (pre-1880s, at 142a Limekiln Lane, when it was called Blackburn's Spirit Vaults). A typical corner local pub which survived until the 1970s. This photographed is from the 1960s, when the manageress was Olga Flannigan. The site is presently open land.
Police Report 1902: Selling drink to a drunken man, 10/- and costs.

Beer House

Listed at 14 Silvester Street (originally Oxford Street North) another street long since rid of its slums. This old Beer House was one of five in the street and lost its licence as long ago as 1906. Photograph from the 1890s, when managed by Annie O'Mahoney. What appears to be an open court entrance is reflected in the window.

St Martin's Cottages

When the atrocious slums of Victorian Liverpool began to be cleared in the 1860s, St Martin's Cottages, in Silvester Street, was the first example in the country of a revolutionary housing design. Erected in 1869 and originally consisting of one hundred and twenty-four tenements in six blocks, the four outer blocks were five storeys high and the two inner blocks three storeys.

Each tenement had a scullery and separate WC and, in two blocks, washing boilers have been provided.

This view of one of the blocks is from 1974, when they were becoming vacant, ready for demolition.

Latimer Arms

This pub was built on the corner of Latimer Street and Ambrose Place. The street still remains but Ambrose Place has long since gone. One of five pubs of the street, the premises was converted to Dining Rooms by 1931. Photograph from 1908, when managed by William Scott.

The following three pubs were, or are, in Hopwood Street. Nine courts once stood here and originally ten pubs.

The Britannia

Listed at 44 Hopwood Street at the junction of Latimer Street. Photographed approximately 1912, when managed by Richard Cross. The original structure closed and was demolished in 1968, when it was managed by Paddy Holligan.

Construction of a new pub commenced on the site immediately. Surrounded by modern housing, it still trades under the original name.

Ship Inn

Situated at the opposite junction of Latimer Street, almost facing the Britannia. It appears as a bare-looking Bent's house in this photograph from the 1950s, when the old housing of Hopwood Street and Latimer Street was still standing. The manager was Samuel Skelland.

The second view shows the premises derelict and burnt out in the early 1990s. It has since been demolished, together with the comparatively modern houses surrounding it.

Clock Vaults

Located at 97 Hopwood Street on the corner of Goodwood Street (originally Cross Street). This pub closed in the 1930s and modern housing now occupies the site. Photographed in 1908, when managed by Horace Tyrer. Entrances to the establishment were in Hopwood Street, Goodwood Street and Back Hopwood Street. Incidentally, Goodwood Street was one of five streets of the vicinity named after race-courses, the other four were: Aintree Street, Ascot Street, Doncaster Street and Epsom Street.

Athol Street is the last street west of Scotland Road before Stanley Road and stretched for approximately one thousand yards, as far as Great Howard Street and is now physically split up from its original line. Originally it contained twenty-six pubs including the following ten.

North Side of Athol Street

The Maid of Erin

On the corner of Darwen Street at 37-39 Athol Street, pre-1880s it was named the Darwen Arms. This photograph was taken in the 1890s, when the pub was managed by Joseph Frayne and the proprietor was Michael Mulcrone. Not listed 1940s.

Written above the window is 'this is Mulchrone's from Great Homer Street' (see the Fleece pub on page 112).

Police Report 1903: Supplying drink to a drunken person, 20/- and costs.

The Cuckoo

This pub was listed as a Beer House before the 1880s and was located at the junction of Paget Street and Athol Street. This photograph was taken in the 1920s, when it was managed by William Barry. The premises was listed as the Atvale Social Club in the 1930s. Next door, at number 47, was a Milk House listed to Peter Cunningham.

Trinity Vaults

Listed at 211 Athol Street and 101 Latimer Street. In the 1860s, the premises had the unusual name of the Chanticleer. This photograph from 1912, was taken when the manager was Robert W Campbell, and shows a former familiar site of old Liverpool – three brass balls, indicating a pawn shop – facing the pub.

It also shows some of the locals congregated on the corner, whilst on the left, in Athol Street, there appears to be a party of school children with their teacher.

The pub has opened and closed a number of times throughout the 1990s, and into the year 2001. Plans are currently underway for the building to be converted into flats. The shops and houses either side have now long gone, with neat, new houses now surrounding the pub, belying a rather gruesome history.

In 1883, just two doors away from the pub at 105 Latimer Street (shown on the photograph), lived Catherine Flanagan, a lodging-house keeper. She and her sister, Margaret Higgins, became known as, 'the Borgias of the slums', after Lucretia Borgia member of an old Italian noble family of Spanish origin, who became notorious as a poisoner.

Whilst living in Skirving Street, they conspired to poison four people, three of them relatives, by using the arsenic from flypaper, (sticky strips that were suspended from the ceiling to attract and kill flies, used in most houses up to the 1950s). After collecting the insurance on the deceased, they moved to Latimer Street, with their crimes apparently undetected.

However, they were soon on the move again, to the nearby Ascot Street. Here, their murderous ways were to continue. Their victim this time, Thomas Higgins, suddenly took ill and, after writhing in excruciating agony all night, died the next day.

His death was certified as being from excessive drinking, but his brother's suspicions were aroused, when he discovered that the deceased had life insurance with no less than six companies. The police were informed and subsequently a post-mortem ordered. This led to the other three bodies being exhumed, to find traces of arsenic in each of them. The two sisters were later tried for murder.

Another murder trial, in 1899, which became internationally famous, was that of American-born, Florence Maybrick, of Aigburth, known as, 'the Flypaper Poisoner'. Although controversial and well-documented, the method she allegedly employed had already been used, some years earlier, by the sisters in question.

Although never gaining the publicity of the Maybrick case, the murder trial of the two sisters was avidly followed locally. Eventually, they were jointly charged with one murder and were hanged at Kirkdale Gaol, during a snow storm, in March 1884.

White Eagle

On the corner of Crompton Street, at 269 Athol Street, this large corner local was managed by Richard Williams when this 1920s shot was taken. Pre-1880s it was called the Eagle Vaults. Not listed 1930s.

Police Report 1892: Permitting drunkenness, dismissed.

South Side

Athol Arms

Situated on the corner of Darwen Street at number 14 Athol Street. Displaying its name on this photograph from 1905, when the pub was managed by Edmond Scott, and the proprietor was Michael Mulcrone (see the Maid of Erin). Pre-1860s it was called the Boiler Maker's Arms. Listed to a Butcher 1940s.

Police Report 1892: Back door opens into closed entry, the door of which, when closed, prevents the police having access to the back door of the public house.

Snowdon Hotel

This pub was at 46-48 Athol Street at the junction of Snowdon Street. Photograph from the 1920s, when the manager was Samuel Swindin. The next door shop was listed to Thomas Byrne, Tobacconist. Not listed 1940s.

Hedley Arms

Occupying 58-62 Athol Street and 64 Hedley Street. Photograph from the 1920s, when managed by John Deeny, with a few customers in the doorway posing for the photographer. The shop next door was listed to August H Loderstedt, Butcher. Listed 1964.
Police Report 1892: Permitting drunkenness, dismissed.

Athol Vaults

Located at 90 Athol Street and 374 Vauxhall Road, the pub presently stands in isolation. The name is just as clearly displayed today, as when photographed in 1908, when managed by John Thornton. The adjoining Tobacconist shop was then listed to Henry Dobson. The shop still remains but is minus its upper storey. The pub is currently standing derelict.
Police Report 1902: Selling drink to a child under 14 years, dismissed. Also: Back door of licensed premises open into enclosed entry, the door of which is closed, prevents the police having free access to the door of the licensed premises.

Beer House

Listed at 122 Athol Street, this old Beer House clearly displaying the manager as Thomas Scally from 1890-1907. No doubt a real scally's pub! The premises was compulsorily purchased in 1924. A rear entrance to the premises led into number 7 Court, Slade Street.

Clock Vaults

Located at the opposite junction of Latimer Street from the Trinity Vaults at 146-148 Athol Street. Photograph from the 1920s, when managed by William Richardson. Premises listed to a Provision Dealer in the 1940s.

Everton

An ancient settlement referred to by name in the 13th century, Everton remained a typical sleepy English village for hundreds of years.

It was during Liverpool's massive expansion in the late 18th and 19th centuries that the town's merchants began to build their impressive town houses and mansions on the steep Everton ridge, offering fine views over the Wirral Peninsula and North Wales.

However, the splendid houses soon gave way to the more humble terraced streets that rapidly spread up and over the slope, wiping away all traces of the gentry who once lived there. Everton's population rose from 4,511 in 1831 to a massive 109,788 by 1881.

In 1835, when Everton became part of Liverpool, the slum-ridden streets of the town had already begun to encroach upon its western side. The visible boundary was all but obliterated by the crowded streets which sprang up, initially within the Liverpool 3 postal district, then spreading into Liverpool 5 and 6.

Being such a huge area, for the purpose of this publication, I am splitting it into two: Liverpool 5 and 6, with a few exceptions. All the following were, or are, in the Liverpool 6 district.

Brunswick Road (originally Folly Lane) is now part of a widened thoroughfare from Islington out of the city centre into West Derby Road. The original frontage has been cleared since the 1970s, with one side landscaped, and the other on the edge of a modern industrial estate.

The following five public houses, from an original thirteen, were on Brunswick Road (none remaining).

Brunswick Arms

This former Higsons' pub was located on the corner of Brunswick Road and Erskine Street. Before the 1880s, it was listed as a Wine and Spirit Vaults. This photograph from the 1950s, shows the pub in the centre, with Erskine Street on the right. The manager at this time was William Edward Highfield. The premises was demolished during the 1970s due to road widening.

A tram-car can be seen turning into Islington from Shaw Street. The block of old Georgian properties to the left of the tram was demolished in 1995 after remaining derelict for many years, despite its listed status. Above the tram, a window in a triangular setting can be seen, this is part of the next featured pub.

The Criterion

Built at the junction of two narrow alleys, the wider of which was called Greenside, the premises, pre-1880s, was listed as a Wine and Spirit Vaults. Its former nickname of Scott's, after Peter Scott who managed the pub from the 1940s to the 1960s, is indicated on the pub's window.

The pub was also locally known as the Irish House, due to the large number of Irishmen who once lodged in nearby Shaw Street and adjacent streets, and who frequented the pub. The adjoining Tobacconist belonged to J Coxhill. Photographed in the 1960s. Listed 1970.

Police Report 1900: Selling drink to a drunken man, to pay costs.

City of London

A former Threlfall's house at 69-71 Brunswick Road, managed by William Harper when photographed in the 1960s. In common with most Threlfall's pubs, it was known locally simply as the Threllies. Pre-1870s it was named the Nag's Head. Listed, 1964.

The arched entrance to the left of the pub formerly led into Tichbourne Terrace, as a *Police Report* from *1903* states – *two entrances in Brunswick Road and one entrance in Tichbourne Terrace.*

The following photograph, from 1935, features Tichbourne Terrace taken from the arch of the City of London.

By the 1960s, when the narrow terrace and court houses had been cleared, the site was used as a car auction lot. It is currently modern housing.

Star of Brunswick

Located at 75 Brunswick Road, at the junction of Starkie Street (originally Duckworth Street), this former Bent's house clearly displayed its name when photographed in approximately 1960. Pre-1860s, it was named the Bull's Head. Listed 1970.

Originally this pub was probably named after the land opposite. During the 1840s the south side of Brunswick Road was only partially built on and was known as the Bull Field, being an old site for the favourite English pastime of bull-baiting. Apparently, a stone post where the bull was tied to await its fate, remained long after the area was built on.

Gregson's Well

Listed at 127-129 Brunswick Road and 1 Radcliffe Street. In this 1960s view a sign reads 'established 1846'. The manager was MJ Byrne. Its name, and that of the pub facing, open to date, make reference to William Gregson, Lord Mayor of Liverpool in 1769, who bought a house hereabouts in 1786. A water well dug on his estate, originally to supply his household and tenants, rapidly became renowned for miles around for its pure water. The overflow formed a stream that ran down the hill behind Brunswick Road. Mr Gregson also had a nearby street named after him. Listed 1970. The above interior view was taken in the 1930s.

This view, from 1955 looking west, features the two Gregson's Wells, with Low Hill veering off to the left. The building in the centre, at the junction of Low Hill and Brunswick Road, formerly the Corner House Café, was earlier a pub, the Phoenix Hotel, which closed in the 1940s. This site is now part of an industrial estate.

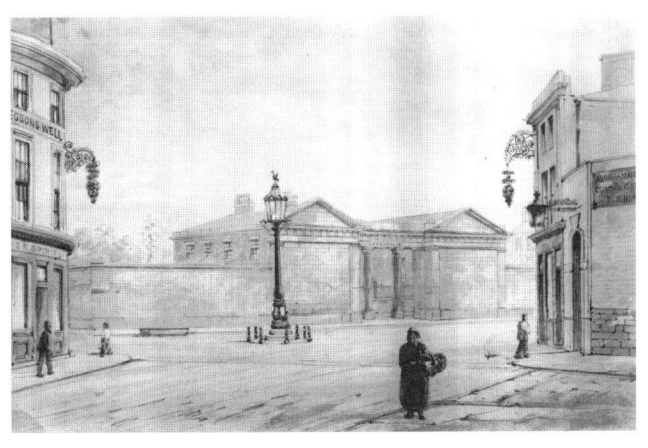

This illustration, from a century earlier, is the reverse view, looking east, towards the Necropolis (city of the dead). This cemetery, opened in 1825, was the first in the town and was an amenity desperately needed, as the population explosion had begun from that period. Previously, burials took place in church graveyards, but these soon became totally inadequate. The cemetery closed in 1898 and, in 1914, the site opened as Grant's Gardens which still remains today. Note what appears to be a Liver bird on top of the light and a horse trough on the road.

Erskine Arms

Situated where Erskine Street meets Epworth Street, before the 1880s it was named the Thespian. The photograph features the former Higsons' house during the 1960s, one of eight former pubs on the street. The pub was demolished in the 1980s and the site has since been fenced off as a different business. The adjoining structures currently remain as the last of the old property on Erskine Street.

Buffalo Arms

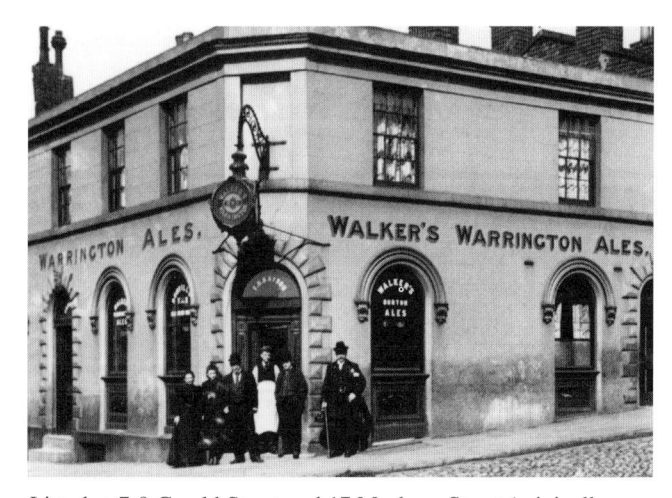

Listed at 7-9 Gerald Street and 17 Meaburn Street (originally Oswald Street), between Brunswick Road and Erskine Street. A modern industrial estate now occupies this site. This appears to be a family photo of the licensee whose name is displayed over the door as FR Rayson, in approximately 1903. Listed 1964.
Police Report 1892: Unjust measure 'excise prosecution', 20/- and 7/6d costs.

Everton Road (originally Everton Lane) runs northward from the top of Brunswick Road and contained eight public houses in living memory, all on its eastern side. Although three existed on the western side, the first, in the 1830s was a Beer House. Later, the Pheasant, located at the junction of Bright Street, was not listed together with the other two by 1908. Ironically, a modern pub, the Hippodrome, now stands close to the original.

The following eight either were, or are, on Everton Road's east side.

The Cheerful Horn

This unusually-named pub stood at the corner of Deacon Street, at number 2 Everton Road and was called The Brook's Hotel pre-1880s. Photographed in the 1890s, when the manageress was Grace Swash, whilst listed as belonging to Richard Lumb, 26 Jasmine Street. This address was a small Brewery located off Heyworth Street, taken over early in the 20th century by Bent's Brewery Co Ltd. The pub closed in the 1930s, later uses included a Chemist, Hosiery Dealer, Money Lender and Licensed Betting Office. The premises was demolished in the 1970s.
Police Report 1903: Domino playing allowed in this house.

Richmond Inn

A former Higsons' house, listed as 32 Everton Road, at the junction of Wren Street (originally Brook's Terrace). The manageress was Harriet Phyllis Kirwan. Note the adjoining landing houses when photographed in the 1960s, also seen on the last photograph. The site of this and the previous pub, together with the landing houses, is now modern housing. Listed 1970.

Neptune Hotel

Listed at number 54 Everton Road, and formerly standing at the junction of Gleave Street, the premises was named the Cannon Vaults before the 1880s. The old, terraced houses of Gleave Street were demolished in the early 1970s and, when rebuilt, the former street and adjacent area was renamed Gleave Square. The huge complex of high-rise flats that replaced them began to fall vacant by the 1990s and they were demolished in 1997. Photographed in approximately 1960, the pub was managed by Frank Edwards and belonged to Birkenhead Ales Brewery. Listed 1970.

Royal Hotel

The next street along from Gleave Street was Mill Road, abolished at Everton Road, with a section remaining east of the former Gleave Square. This former Ind-Coope house was listed at 78 Everton Road and 1-3 Mill Road. Listed 1970. The pub was known locally as Hartleys.
Police Report 1903: Prosecuted for permitting music and singing on Christmas Day, dismissed.

Masonic Arms

This former large Tetley's pub, at number 84 Everton Road, was situated on the corner of Cresswell Street, the next street along from Mill Road. The previous pub, the Royal, can also be seen in this photograph from the 1960s, when the manager was William Sutherland. Listed 1970. The site is now modern housing.

The Clarence

The only pub currently remaining on Everton Road's east side, at number 92. Photographed in the mid-1960s when a Higsons' house and managed by Edward Wise, whose surname supplied the pub's nickname. The premises now stands in isolation at the junction with Spencer Street. The adjoining shops were Irene's Hairdressers and TJ Milligan, Ophthalmic Optician.
Police Report 1903: Selling drink to a drunken woman, 20/- and costs.

Cumberland

Two streets northward, on the corner of Lloyd Street (abolished), at number 106 Everton Road. This pub was a Beer House pre-1890s. When photographed in approximately 1960, the licensee was James Hickey, and the pub was known locally as Bill Robbo's. The adjoining shop was a Provision Merchants – Perry and Rouston. Listed 1964. The site is currently the Provincial Club.

Clock

Adjoining Lloyd Street stood Hodson Place (realigned) on which corner this pub was located at 116 Everton Road. Before the 1880s, it was named the Village Clock. In the early 1960s, when this photograph was taken, the manager was Sidney Reginald Morgan and the premises was known locally as Camerons. The adjoining shop belonged to J Hitcham, Grocer. Listed 1964.

On the corner of Everton Road and Aubrey Street was an extremely large building, housing various licensed and unlicensed premises over the years. These included: 1890s Everton Conservative Club Ltd; 1908 Dancing School; 1930s Douro Athletic, Football and Social Club and Princes United Social and Football Club; 1950s Everton Ward Labour Club.

The following were located in a former maze of terraced streets north of Brunswick Road and west of Everton Road, all demolished during the 1960s and 70s.

The Red Lamp

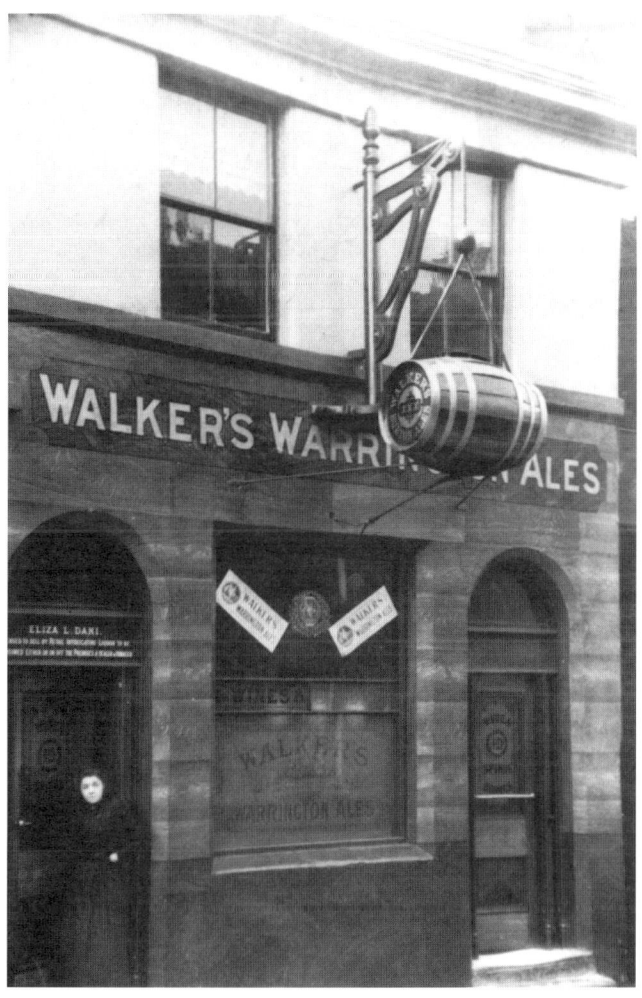

This was listed at 25, in the now non-existent Starkie Street, with a rear entrance in Westbourne Street. A former Beer House, clearly indicating the licensee's name as Eliza L Dani (Elizabeth Love; probably the woman in the doorway). Photographed in 1905. The pub closed in the 1920s.

Pre-1860s, when Starkie Street was named Duckworth Street, another pub, the Woolpack was at number 11, which later became the Myrtle Cottage in the 1880s and finally the Alma Vaults, which closed in the 1930s. The name Woolpack was one of the earliest given to a public house throughout the country. For centuries the wool industry was the backbone of England's prosperity and actually accounted for half the value of land of the whole country in the 13th century.

Beer House

A typical old Beer House listed at 30 Alma Street, formerly the continuation of Starkie Street. In common with many former beer houses, the pub was simply part of a terraced house. Advertising Bass's Guinness in the window and managed by John Westgarth when photographed in the 1890s, it had ceased trading by 1908.
Police Report 1903: Selling drink to a drunken man, £5 0s 0d and costs, licence endorsed and quoit playing allowed in this house.

Boars Head

Situated at the junction of Bright Street and Cobden Street. Photographed in the 1960s when managed by Richard Emmanuel Fitzgerald (shown in this view) and known locally as Richie's.

The site and vicinity of this pub was replaced in the early 1970s by a new housing estate known as the Radcliffe Estate. It rapidly became a prime example of the architectural blunders so common throughout the city in the 1960s and 70s. The houses themselves were fine but the design of the narrow walkways at ground level and above, together with a maze of staircases and blind alleys, quickly earned the estate its reputation as a mugger's paradise. So rapid was the decline of the estate, that it was demolished a mere ten years after construction. It is somewhat ironic that whilst the estate was so short-lived, the pub had existed for over a century. John O'Brien, a friend of mine, recalls the following:

'Past customers of the Boar's Head would agree that it was a pub not lacking in characters and an establishment that has probably gone down in the annals of history as a pub that time passed by. It was just a working man's pub noted for its "stay behinds" and frequented by people from the local community. Amongst the regulars, there were men known as "tatters" who eked out a living by going around the area looking for scrap, where it was abundant, as the district was under demolition and tumbling down, particularly during the 1960s and early 1970s.

The manager, Richie Fitz, although small in stature, was a giant in generosity. Like many people of the day, he was one of many voluntary "social workers" who looked after the less fortunate of the community. He was also a man with a sense of humour. One night a drunk threw a house brick through the pub window. The following day the offending brick was on the counter labelled, "Exhibit A".

In my opinion, when the pub was closed and demolished, an epitaph saying "God bless the Boar's Head and all who aled in her!" should have been erected on the site.'

Police Report 1892: Permitting music and singing on Good Friday, 5/- and costs. Also, quoit and domino playing allowed in this house.

Prince of Wales

Formerly standing at the junction of Gregson Street and Bright Street, this was one of five pubs of the vicinity. Before the 1880s, the premises was a Wine and Spirit Vaults. This photograph is from the early 1960s. Listed 1964.

Police Report 1903: Licensed for music and singing, on condition that there is no free and easy and that the licence is only occasionally made use of and a snug off the bar is difficult of police supervision.

The following two pubs were in Plumpton Street (named after Samuel Plumpton, who owned land in the vicinity).

Eagle Inn

Listed at the junction of Guilford Street (abolished) and Plumpton Street. Photographed in 1905 when managed by Alice Potter. Not listed 1920s.

Police Report 1903: Quoit playing allowed.

Beer House

A typical, bare-looking, unnamed Beer House from pre-First World War Liverpool, standing at the junction of a tiny cul-de-sac named St George's Terrace (abolished). The licence was revoked in 1911. This photograph is from the 1890s, when managed by Elizabeth Connor, probably the lady in the doorway.

Police Report 1892: Selling drink to a drunken woman, 4/6 and costs.

Beer House

Standing at the corner of Guilford Street and Wilmott Street (abolished), this Beer House was photographed in 1908 when the manager was Roger Parker. Just visible on the left are some landing houses. Its licence was revoked in 1911. Premises reopened during the 1920s as the Guilford Arms, when managed by Alfred Watts. Listed 1964.

The above view shows Wilmott Terrace, Wilmott Street during the 1930s and the landing houses that were once abundant throughout the inner city. The previous pub can be partly seen at the top left-hand corner. The street was cleared during the 1960s.

The next district covered in this vicinity is the area north of West Derby Road, east of Everton Road, south of Breck Road and west of Belmont Road. The following three pubs, from an original eight, were, or are, on Mill Road.

Sefton Arms

Listed at 68 Mill Road and 65 Lavan Street (abolished). The site of this and the next pub is now an enclosed, grassed area. Off the nearby Caird Street is a modern cul-de-sac named Lavan Close. The pub was photographed in the early 1960s when still open and managed by Annie Brown. Listed 1964.
Police Report 1903: Quoit playing allowed.

Wellington Hotel

Listed at 78a Mill Road and 55 Caird Street, the photograph shows a customer on his way in for a pint during the 1960s, when managed by Elizabeth Kane. Listed 1970.

Grapes Hotel

Standing where Mill Road meets Margaret Street, the Grapes Hotel is one of only two pubs to survive to date on what has been generally referred to as the Queens Road Estate since the early 1970s (see Whitefield Road, page 86). In the 1960s, when this view was taken, the Grapes was a Threlfall's pub, managed by Richard Hughes. The premises has closed and reopened on a number of occasions throughout the 1990s, and into 2001 is standing in derelict isolation.

The following three pubs, from a total of eight, were in Spencer Street, so named, together with Steers Street, after Spencer James Steers, a grandson of Thomas Steers, the renowned dock engineer who owned land hereabouts.

The Quadrant

A huge former corner public house on the corner of Spencer Street and Steers Street (originally Elbow Lane) situated a little behind the present Clarence pub on Everton Road. Photographed in 1908, when the licensee was Simon Smith. The pub closed through a compulsory purchase order in 1919. *Police Report 1903: The door in the side passage is difficult of supervision.*

Baths Hotel

Named after a former swimming baths that once stood in Margaret Street, now replaced by new houses. Both streets still remain, with a mixture of houses built in the 1960s and 70s, together with more recently-built houses. Photographed in the 1920s when the manager was Alfred Pugh. Listed 1964.

This view shows Aubrey Street (realigned) in 1955. The water tower of the Everton Water Works is featured to the left of the number 19 tram, en route to the Pier Head. Work started on the underground reservoir in 1854 by Thomas Duncan, the Corporation's first water engineer (see Whitefield Road, page 86). Just behind, is St Chrysostom's (now replaced with a modern church). Before the 1970s, the street was a major thoroughfare, running eastward from Everton Road. At the junction with Queens Road the trams, and later, buses, turned north to join Breck Road. The building centre-right, beyond a former taxi office, is the Swan Hotel, featured overleaf.

The Shakespeare

A former Ind-Coope pub standing at the junction of Shakespeare Street. Since the new estate was built, a tiny section of old Shakespeare Street remains off Atwell Street, facing the modern Shakespeare Way. Photographed approximately 1960, when managed by Alfred Odgen. Listed 1970.

Police Report 1892: Quoit playing allowed in this house.

The following two pubs, from an original four, were in Aubrey Street.

Swan Hotel

Trading at the junction of Belgrave Terrace and Aubrey Street, and bearing the name Duncan's, after Mary Duncan, the manageress, when this picture was taken in the 1890s.

What appears to be an advertisement for a proposed competition between Everton and Salford is displayed in the window, although, as the rest of the writing is illegible, a fixture, or indeed the sport, cannot be identified.

The premises closed in the 1950s, last trading as a furniture manufacturer before demolition in the 1960s.
Police Report 1903: Card playing carried out in this house.

Audley Arms

Located in the section of the thoroughfare east of Queens Road, which was just a side street, at the corner of Shakespeare Street, this pub was known locally as Joe's. Photographed approximately 1960. Listed 1970.
Police Report 1902: Card playing allowed in this house.

Queens

Located at 75 Queens Road, (formerly one of three pubs of Queens Road), at the junction of Spencer Street, whose large, three storey houses are shown. Photographed during the 1960s, when the manager was Leslie Albert Michael Norris, this pub avoided the mass demolition of the vicinity during the 1960s and 70s, only to close in 1992. Vandals then moved in and the pub was inevitably demolished.

Dolphin Hotel

Situated at 7 Sarah Street, between Aubrey Street and Lloyd Street. The manager during the 1960s, when this shot was taken, was John Leslie McConnell. Listed 1970.
Police Report 1892: Domino and quoits played.

The Cottage

Listed at 1 Dawber Street at the corner of Whitefield Terrace off Whitefield Road. Mrs Violet Irene Hawkins was manageress during the 1960s when photographed. Before the 1890s, the pub was named the Whitefield Inn. Listed 1970.
Police Report 1898: Supplying liquor to a police constable while on duty, dismissed.

The following two pubs, from an original three, were in Kilshaw Street.

Kilshaw Vaults

Located at 101 Kilshaw Street on the corner of Atwell Street and managed by Janet Eccles when this photograph was taken in approximately 1960. Both streets now contain modern housing. Listed 1964.
Police Report 1903: Former licensee summoned for obstructing the police, 5/- and costs. Domino playing allowed in this house.

Beer House

This old Beer House was named the City Vaults before closure in 1919. Listed as a dairy in the 1920s. It appears that the pub was added to the terraced property in Kilshaw Street after the construction of the street, which was built during the 1850s and 60s. Advertising London Stout and Sparkling Ales in the window when photographed in 1905 when managed by Emily Trainor.
Police Report 1903: Card and parlour quoit playing allowed.

Boundary Vaults

Listed at 80a Boundary Lane, one of eight former pubs. Photographed during the 1890s when Andrew Kennedy was the manager. The adjoining Boundary Hall is advertising 'Dancing Academy – dancing, piano and violin taught'. Premises closed in the 1950s, when it was taken over by an Electrical Contractor.

When open, the pub was known locally as the Black House, due to the pub being in almost total darkness in parts. The pub was still lit by gaslight, with some parts obviously lacking gas mantles. Also known as Farrell's, after a former manager.

The Grapes

The Grapes was formerly listed at 2 Reynolds Street and 1-3 Severs Street, two of the former densely-congested streets of the vicinity. This view is from 1912, when the manager was Joseph Heritage. Severs Street is now a mixture of industrial premises and housing, whilst Reynolds Street was abolished along its original line and a neat new housing development, named Reynolds Close, now occupies the site. The pub was known locally as Mad Dan's. Listed 1964.
Police Report 1903: Card playing carried on in this house. The door and side passage is difficult of supervision.

Beer House

This bare-looking pub was closed under compulsory purchase as long ago as 1905. Formerly at 34 Knowsley Street, at the corner of Greenwood Street, off Boundary Lane. The site is currently open grassland behind modern housing.
Police Report 1903: Quoit playing allowed in this house.

Prior to the 1970s, Whitefield Road ran from Breck Road in an irregular line through what is now the Queens Road Estate, then across Boundary Lane/Breckfield Road South, as far as Belmont Road - this section remaining. The section between Breck Road and Boundary Lane/Breckfield Road South was originally named Whitefield Lane, with the remainder named Round Hill Lane.

Fourteen pubs once lined Whitefield Road including the following nine.

The Whitefield

Before the 1880s this pub was named the Wellington Hotel. Currently, it is one of only two original pubs on the estate. The above view is from the 1960s, when the manager was Marion Hodge. A former back alley adjoining the pub, named Back Shakespeare Street, can be clearly seen.

The view above shows a typical scene from 1994 where, as also featured on the next but one view, housing built only some 20 years earlier, has since been demolished.

The premises was originally at 90 Whitefield Road but, with the on-going renovation of the area, it is now listed in Whitefield Way. The pub has opened and closed at various times of late and is currently closed.

Police Report 1903: Domino playing allowed.

Reservoir Vaults

Aptly-named, due to its former position on the corner of Brunel Street and Whitefield Road, facing the Everton Water Works, which still stands as a well-known local landmark. Pre-1880s, the pub was named the John Bull Vaults. When photographed in the 1960s, the manager was John Carroll, and the pub was known locally as Mrs Henshaw's. Listed 1970. A modern pub, aptly named the Brunel, now stands close to the original.

Police Report 1892: Quoits playing, carried on in this house.

During the 1990s, this vicinity, known as the Queen's Road Estate, was in the process of either renovation or demolition, neither of which should have been necessary for housing only two to three decades old. Sadly, this is a common occurrence throughout all the older parts of the city. This view, from 1994, shows the approximate location of the previous pub, including the high level tank of the Everton Water Works. This was built in 1857 to hold 2,700 gallons and stands 90 feet in height.

The following were, or are, on the section of Whitefield Road that remains as a thoroughfare from Breckfield Road South/Boundary Lane to Belmont Road.

St Albans

Listed at 97 Whitefield Road (earlier number 1), this huge pub, standing at the junction of Breckfield Road South, was aptly-known as the Roundhouse. Harold Currie was manager at the time of this 1960s photograph. Listed 1970.

A modern pub, the Strawberry (currently closed), now occupies the site. This name is taken from an old inn, the Strawberry Tavern, formerly located a little south of this location (see West Derby Road).
Police Report 1900: Selling drink to a drunken man, dismissed on payment of costs.

The George

Listed at 129 Whitefield Road (earlier 33) on the corner of St Albans (which still remains). I wondered why the former pub, and not this one, was named St Albans. Apparently, it was because this pub was named The George pre-1880s, when at 33 Round Hill Lane, with the St Albans at number 1. Both were in existence before the street was laid out.

John Thomas managed the pub when the following photograph was taken in the early 1960s. Listed 1970.
Police Report 1892: Selling drink to a drunken man, 4/6 and costs.

Woodville

Located at 153 Whitefield Road and 107 Woodville Terrace. In the 1960s, this pub was known locally as Sue's; the licensee being Susan Mary Fitzgerald. Listed 1970.
Police Report 1892: Parlour quoit playing allowed in this house.

Rock Light

Trading at the junction of Grey Rock Street and Whitefield Road, this pub was named the Rock Hotel before the 1890s. In the 1970s, the building was replaced by new housing. The photograph shows the pub in the 1920s when the manager was John Otterson. The pub was known locally as May's. Listed 1964.

Peel Arms

The only pub currently open on this section of Whitefield Road, is listed at 165 at the corner of Franklin Place. The 1980s photograph shows the derelict former factory of Barker and Dobsons, at the other side of Franklin Place, which has since been replaced by a housing estate. In the mid 19th century a pub named the Spotted Cow stood in Franklin Place.
Police Report 1903: Selling drink to a drunken man, dismissed.

The Newbie

The Newbie was situated where Whitefield Road meets Underhill Street (abolished). The site is now part of a small industrial estate. It was photographed in approximately 1960, when the licensee was Mary Agnes Welsh, with the pub known locally as Aggie's. Listed 1970.

Horn of Plenty

A uniquely-named former pub listed at 250 Whitefield Road, at the junction of Whiteford Street. Photographed in the 1920s when the licensee was Mrs Sarah O'Connell. Listed 1964.

This unusual name derives from Cornucopia – Horn of Plenty, represented as a goat's horn overflowing with flowers, fruit and corn. Horn is also an ancient name for a drinking cup.

The Cupid

This former Bent's pub was listed at 2 Cupid Street (abolished) which, pre-1980s, was off Belmont Road at the junction of Larch Lea. The manager in this 1960s photograph was Albert Leach. The site is now part of an industrial estate. Listed 1970.

The Red Rock

Located in one of the Rock Streets, at 42 Red Rock Street, between Whitefield Road and West Derby Road. In 1903 the entrances to this establishment were described as follows: 2 in Red Rock Street, 1 in Cart Passage at side. The pub was known locally as Crosbie's. Listed 1964, this view is from that period.

Harewood

Almost facing Red Rock Street, on the other side of Whitefield Road, stood Harewood Street, where this establishment was located at the junction with Pickering Street, now the site of a car park. Photographed in the 1960s when managed by Lillian Pain whose surname was the pub's nickname. Listed 1970.

Lord Clive

Standing at 63 Belmont Road at the corner of Allen Street (abolished), this was one of four original pubs. A former Bent's house, it was demolished in the 1980s. Photographed in approximately 1970, when the manager was F Cant.

Lido

The Lido was a former cinema of Belmont Road. Although still displaying its name in this 1960s view, it had in fact closed in 1959 and was in use as a warehouse when photographed. The Cinema had opened in 1914, as the Belmont Road Picture House, becoming the Lido Cinema in 1938.

Circa 1970 the premises was converted to a theatre club and cabaret named the Wookey Hollow which remained a well-known city night club until the early 1980s when it closed due to fire damage. During the 1980s, the premises reopened briefly as two separate pubs, the Wookey and Barney Rubble's, since when the building has remained closed until 2001 and is finally undergoing renovation.

We now leave this locality and return to Brunswick Road, where it continues eastward at Everton Road, to become West Derby Road (originally Rake Lane), a major thoroughfare to Tuebrook and West Derby. Although the current West Derby village area (featured), now a suburb of Liverpool, is quite a distance from here, the remainder of this section was not strictly Everton but West Derby.

Liverpool was surrounded by four townships before municipal boundary changes in the 19th century. They were Kirkdale, Everton, West Derby and Toxteth Park. West Derby, formerly an ancient and important township, comprised the remainder of this section (Liverpool 6) and included the adjoining Edge Hill area (Liverpool 7), as far as Toxteth Park. The major part of the frontage on both sides of West Derby Road, on the section between Everton Road and Belmont Road, has been cleared since the 1970s.

The north side of the road, on this section alone, contained 25 licensed premises, the majority of which, somewhat surprisingly, being within living memory. including the following nineteen.

The following either are, or were, on this section of the road, on the north side of West Derby Road.

Strawberry Tavern

One of the earliest pubs on the road, the Strawberry Tavern was formerly located near the site of the present St Michael's Church and north of the Parrot pub. When this tavern existed in the mid-19th century, it was in a rural location, set back from the road with open countryside running eastward.

Elaborate gardens existed around the inn as far as Hygeia Street westward, and Boundary Lane eastward. Although named the Strawberry Tavern, it appears that strawberries were never grown there. Also called the Strawberry Bank on various lists.

As the ever-expanding town was built up eastward along West Derby Road, the surrounding gardens were gradually swept away, although the premises and land did not vanish overnight. A portion of the gardens became the West Derby Hospital (not to be confused with the nearby West Derby Union Workhouse, later Mill Road Hospital) later to become St George's Industrial School.

Northward, the large Ogden's tobacco factory, extending from Hygeia Street to Boundary Lane, took over the bulk of the land. This remains open to date, although now a much smaller, modern building.

On Boundary Lane, a section of the old gardens was also replaced by Haig's Brewery in the 1870s. Thomas Haig seems to have acquired the inn some time before closure in the 1890s, as he was listed as the registered owner at that time.

One of its last licensees was former boxer, Jem Mace, born in Beeston, Norfolk in 1831. He was one of the world's greatest bare knuckle fighters but lived to see the transition to gloves. Principally a welterweight, he nevertheless often fought much heavier opponents.

His career, which spanned thirty-five years, from 1855 to 1890, is in the Guinness Book of Records as the longest of any boxer. He won his first championship in 1861, beating Sam Hurst. He lost it again in 1862, but regained it in 1866, stopping Joe Goss in twenty-one rounds. In May 1870, when approaching the age of forty, he won a world title fight in America, beating Tom Allen in Louisiana.

After retiring and taking over the pub, Jem Mace organised boxing and sparring festivals, as well as teaching his craft to other young hopefuls. Although he died in Jarrow-on-Tyne in 1910, he was buried in Anfield Cemetery, Liverpool.
Police Reports 1892: Supplying drink to a drunken man, dismissed. Side door opens onto a plot of land enclosed by a wooden hoarding and a back door onto a plot of land enclosed by a brick wall. At the last annual licence sessions, the licence was renewed on condition that the doors of the above enclosures were closed up. This has not been done.

York Hotel

Before the 1880s this local was called the Star, and was situated at number 3-5 West Derby Road, at the corner of Aber Street. A former Bent's house, it was a well-frequented pub of the town, known as the Bass House and, as clearly indicated on the pub, was particularly known for its draught Bass. Photographed approximately 1960, when the manager was Charles Sunderland. The site is currently open land. Listed 1970.
Police Report 1903: Prosecuted for selling spirits without licence, £13 and costs (excise prosecution).

George Hotel

Located at the corner of Ogwen Street, at number 19 West Derby Road, and known as the Barrel House, this pub was named the Prince of Wales Hotel in the 1880s, and Lloyd's Hotel up to 1898. The site is now open land. This view was taken in the 1960s, when the pub was managed by Edward Francis Ryan. The adjoining shop was listed to CE Aspinall, Newsagent. Listed 1970.
Police Report 1898: The back door leads into a yard. One stall of the stable is sublet.

The Brougham

Situated on the corner of Caird Street, at number 39a West Derby Road. The pub was called the Lord Brougham, pre-1890s, after the facing Brougham Terrace which, in turn, was named after Henry Peter, first Baron Brougham, a former Lord Chancellor of England (see Royal Standard, page 96). The premises was demolished in the 1980s and the site of the pub is currently grassland, with Caird Street still a thoroughfare. Managed by Michael Gannon during the early 1960s when this shot was taken. The adjoining shop was Sayers Confectioners.

Dunkeld Arms

Located at the junction of Dunkeld Street (abolished), at 53a West Derby Road. This former Tetley's pub, photographed in the 1960s, when the manageress was Ivy Lily Hannon, was known locally as Jack Hannon's and also for a while as the Old Maid's Pub. Pre-1890s it was named the Gordon Arms. Surprisingly, although closing in 1974, the premises remained derelict for just over 20 years, until its demolition in 1995, leaving the adjoining Furniture Store currently trading in isolation.

Clock Hotel

Pre-1880s known as the Royal Clock. A former Greenall's pub at 81 West Derby Road, at the corner of Lynedoch Street. This mid-1960s photograph also shows M & L Cars Ltd, Second Hand Car Dealers and, adjoining the pub, Mark's Hairdressers. The premises was demolished in the 1980s, with the street abolished and the site now a garage.

Olympia Hotel

Listed at 99-101 West Derby Road and 2 Hughes Street, the Olympia Hotel is one of only three pubs currently open on this section of the road. In this 1960s photograph, the pub was a Threlfall's house with W Costigan, Grocers, adjoining.

I was informed that tunnels formerly ran from the pub, under West Derby Road, to the former Olympia Theatre, which opened in 1905 and Hengler's Circus, (later the Hippodrome Theatre, described in Volume 1) and that many of the theatrical stars stayed in the pub whilst performing there. The pub was renamed after the theatre and its upper rooms still have numbers on the doors. It was previously called the Grapes.

In 1925 the theatre was converted to a cinema and became famous throughout the city as the first in Liverpool to feature 'talkies' – the first film was *The Singing Fool* starring Al Jolson, in 1929. However, with other cinemas rapidly acquiring the new technology, and competition fierce, the premises closed in 1939.

After the War, a new generation frequented the building when it became the Locarno Ballroom. Then, in 1964, with the game of bingo becoming very popular, the ballroom was converted into a bingo hall. After a long period of closure, it was opened once again as the Olympia Theatre in March 2000.

Incidentally, before the Olympia was built, the site was listed in the 1860s as the Licensed Victuallers Asylum, as the Licensed Victuallers Institution by the 1870s, and from the 1880s until demolition about 1902, as the Licensed Victuallers Cottages and Association.

VALUABLE
FREEHOLD LICENSED PREMISES
— IN —
West Derby Road, Liverpool.

To be Sold by Auction,

— BY —

MR. WILLIAM THOMSON,

If not previously disposed of by Private Treaty.

On Wednesday, the 22nd October, 1890,

AT THREE P.M. PRECISELY, AT THE

LAW ASSOCIATION ROOMS, 14 COOK ST., LIVERPOOL,

Subject to Conditions of Sale to be then produced :

ALL THAT FREEHOLD

FULLY - LICENSED PUBLIC - HOUSE,

AND PREMISES,

SITUATE AT THE

Corner of West Derby Road and Hughes Street,

And being Nos. 99 and 101 in West Derby Road, and No. 2 in Hughes Street. The Premises have a frontage of about 33 feet to West Derby Road and 63 feet to Hughes Street, and contain in the whole about 220 Square Yards of Land.

The Premises are situated in one of the leading thoroughfares of Liverpool, and are in the midst of a thickly populated neighbourhood.

The Property is offered subject to an existing tenancy, which expires on the 20th day of December, 1891.

For further particulars apply to the AUCTIONEER, 7 Cook Street, Liverpool; ALEXANDER COLLINS, Esq., Harrington Street, Solicitor; or to

Messrs. BATESON, WARR & BATESON, Solicitors,

14 CASTLE STREET, LIVERPOOL.

The Parrot

This decorative pub at the junction of Hygeia Street, boasted two statues on its facade. William Ryder was the manager when photographed in 1903. Also shown is an adjoining cocoa rooms, listed as the British Workman Public House Co Ltd, which closed in the 1920s.

This pub had its origins way back in the 1830s, when a large house existed at the junction of Hygeia Street and Rake Lane (later West Derby Road). A zoological gardens had opened opposite in 1832, with the entrance facing Hygeia Street (see end of West Derby Road). A Mr William Mayman, who resided in the house in question, acquired a job as a keeper in the zoo. He became something of a local hero when he was injured rescuing a young boy who was being mauled by an escaped bear. As a reward for his brave deed, a subscription was raised, which resulted in him opening part of his house as a pub. He commissioned a sign which read, 'Mayman in the Jaws of the Bear' which apparently attracted quite a clientele and, by 1843, the premises was licensed as the Man and Bear.

By the 1850s, when the licensee was a Mr Mitchell, the name had been changed to the Parrot, then at 181. The premises shown in the second view may have been added onto the original house, or rebuilt in the 1860s, as from then on it was listed at 127 West Derby Road.

This 1960s view, when the manager was Joseph Ainsworth, shows the former Cocoa Rooms, then listed to Low & Co, Builders Merchants and, at 131, Crown Fireplace Specialists. Adjoining the pub, in Hygeia Street, was TKS Motor Engineering. Part of Ogden's Tobacco Works can be seen in the background. Listed 1964.

The Killarney

This pub, formerly at 139 West Derby Road, was at the junction of Horne Street, which is only 67 yards long. Pre-1880s it was called the Niagara Vaults. The railings of St Michael's RC Church, which still stands on the opposite corner, can be seen in this 1970s view. William Brough was manager at this time and, quite justifiably, the pub was known as the Catholic House. The adjoining shops were RA Owen Confectioners at 141, Guyles Turf Accountants at 143 and Magee's Outfitters at 145. The whole block is now part of Ogden's Tobacco Works.
Police Report 1892: Selling drink to a drunken man, dismissed.

Albert

At 163 West Derby Road, at the corner of Heber Street, also destined to be swallowed up by Ogden's. Anne Logan managed the pub when photographed in the late 1960s and, like the previous pub, her full name was adopted as the pub's local title. The adjoining shops were Hardie & Co, Wine and Spirit Merchant at 165 and Parry's Ladies and Children's Wear at 167. Listed 1970.

The Albion

The next street was Tooke Street, only 60 yards long, at the corner of which the Albion stood at 151, known for a time as the Shakes. The street was engulfed by Ogden's Tobacco Works and disappeared. The adjoining shop was a branch office of the Daily Post and Echo, with the next shop, a former newsagents, closed in this 1960s picture. Emma Hughes managed the pub and it was known locally by her name. Listed 1970.

The Newsham

Ogden's factory ends at Boundary Lane, which is still a main thoroughfare. The Newsham Hotel, at 183 West Derby Road, stood at the other junction and is now replaced by landscaping in front of St Michael's Club. In this photograph from the 1960s, the adjoining shops were Mrs EM Hartley's Tobacconists at 185 and WG Walker's Grocery at 187. The pub's manager at the time was William Edward Fairclough. Note the old fire alarm on West Derby Road. Listed 1964.

New Boundary

Listed as 195-197 West Derby Road, originally occupying the junction of Grey Rock Street, the site is now covered with modern housing. Photographed during the 1960s when Mary Hughes was licensee and by whose full name the pub was known. The adjoining shops were JK Donnelly, Confectioner and Melias, Grocers. Listed 1970.

Sheil Park Hotel

A former Threlfall's pub at the junction of Red Rock Street, at 207 West Derby Road. The site now contains modern housing. Managed by John Cackett during the 1960s, when this photograph was taken. The adjoining shop was listed to BD Loggie, Newsagents. Listed 1964.

Eureka Hotel

A Walker's house at 217 West Derby Road, at the junction of the third of the Rock Streets; White Rock Street. Like the previous pub, new housing occupies this site. This view is from 1909, when the manager was Thomas Overington. The streets were named after the nature of the rock and the modern estate retains the old names of Red, White and Grey Rock. Listed 1970.

The Saxon

This former Walker's pub, which stood at the corner of Saxon Street (abolished), has also been replaced by new housing. This view is from the early 1970s, when it was at number 241 West Derby Road. Adjoining was M Lewis, Fruit Retailer and Bernard J Rooney, Licensed Broker. Listed 1970.

Norwood Arms

A former Higsons' house at 263 West Derby Road, occupying a site at the corner of Goth Street (abolished), was listed as a Beer House pre-1880s. This shot is from the 1960s, when the manager was Margaret Arnold. The adjoining shop was listed to Miss E Ball, Hardware Store. Modern housing now occupies the site. Listed 1970.

Police Report 1903: Selling drink to a drunken man, dismissed.

Grapes

This Bent's house, at 277 West Derby Road, was managed by Frederick James Brown when photographed in the 1960s. It is the second pub still open along this section of the road. The junction at Celt Street, where it stands, is all but demolished and the pub is still known locally as the Celt.

The Belmont

Listed at 303 West Derby Road and 1a Belmont Road, this is the last pub open on this section of the road. The pub displays a date of 1885, but a pub with the same name is listed in the 1860s. Photograph from the 1970s, when managed by Frederick Wynne. The adjoining shops on Belmont Road have since been demolished. They were L McAndrew Ltd, Confectioners, Mrs Annie Jones, Wardrobe Dealer, TG Foster Ltd, Chemists and P & W Soft Furnishings. Taylor's Newsagent & Tobacconist shown on West Derby Road is still trading.

Considering the huge number of pubs on the north side of West Derby Road, only six were, or are, within living memory, on the south side.

2-4	Gregson's Well, corner of Low Hill, open to date.
86	Derby Arms, corner of Farnworth Street, open to date.
88	Cyprus Hotel, corner of Farnworth Street. Listed 1964.
160	Dee Vaults, corner of Dee Street (known as Mrs James'). Listed 1964.
192-194	Boundary, corner of Palatine Street. Listed 1964.

... and the following one:

Royal Standard

This pub, at 16 West Derby Road on the corner of Walker Street, was named the Scawfell Hotel pre-1890s. This view is from the late 1980s and shows part of Brougham Terrace to the left. The wall to the right formed part of the former Hippodrome Cinema. The pub is currently closed, despite recent renovation.

Berwick Hotel

Formerly located in one of the streets off the south side of West Derby Road, at 67 Berwick Street, at the corner of Proctor Street. In this early 1970s photograph, prior to demolition, the high-rise flats off Sheil Road loom in the background. The site is currently landscaped.

Just over 30 years after construction, the high-rise flats of Sheil Road are undergoing demolition. This view from 1998 shows the approximate site of West Derby Road/Berwick Street, where the previous pub was located.

The continuation of West Derby Road, at its junction with Belmont Road, is named Rocky Lane but it becomes West Derby Road again at Lower Breck Road. It is here, still in Liverpool 6, that the Newsham Park Hotel at 425 (pre-1920s, 305) long known locally as the Birkenhead House and the Park Hotel listed at 495 (pre-1920s, 403), can be found. The remainder of West Derby Road is in Tuebrook, Liverpool 13, where three pubs stood that each had Tuebrook in their name, including the following two:

Tuebrook Inn

Situated where West Derby Road meets New Road, at number 266, this local was demolished in approximately 1970 to make way for road improvements. This picture is from the 1920s, when the manager was William Carty. The adjoining shop was listed to D Higgins, Butchers.

The Tuebrook

The Tuebrook, at number 583 West Derby Road, is open to date and has adopted its former nickname – the Flat House. In the 1920s it was managed by Norman Robinson, probably the man standing in the doorway. The adjoining Ironmongers shop belonged to Edwin Watson.

The third pub featuring the name Tuebrook was the Tuebrook Hotel at 268 West Derby Road, on the corner of New Road. Listed 1970.

One of West Derby Road's former pubs, the Little Talbot, was to be found at 150. Before the 1860s it was known as the Zoological Vaults, named after a former zoological garden which flourished here for just over 30 years from 1832, before being engulfed by the encroaching tide of terraced property, stretching westward from what was to become Butler Street, to Farnworth Street. In the 1930s, the pub was listed to a Hardware Dealer.

A long-forgotten Beer House of the road was to be found at 236, which, pre-1880s, was listed to Thomas Phillips, Importer of American Oysters. Not listed by 1908.

Leaving this locality, I now turn to the vicinity south of West Derby Road, starting at Low Hill. The following were, or are, in Low Hill, which had eight pubs.

In the following three photographs, the changing face of the Low Hill and Kensington junction can be seen.

Beer House

This Beer House, at 2 Low Hill, was photographed in approximately 1905, when the manager was William Hall. Adjoining, at number 4, was William Disley, Dairyman (his surname partly shown above Cow Keeper on the facia). The Beer House ceased trading in the 1920s. The former common practice having street names on the glass of the gas-lamp, is featured as Low Hill & Kensington.

The above photograph shows the Beer House in approximately 1950, when it was in use as a fish shop, with number 4 not listed. The Coach and Horses, next door at number 6, was then managed by Randall McDonald. A large advertisement, stretching across 2 and 4, displays a local taxi firm which was located lower down Kensington. The Beer House and adjacent building were demolished in the late 1950s, leaving its neighbour the Coach and Horses standing in isolation.

The premises on Kensington, all demolished, were Miss Annie Tweedale, Newsagent, Samuel Black, Secondhand Boot Dealer, Albert Hancox, Tobacconist and Autolux Taxi Service.

Coach and Horses

This view, from the 1970s, shows the Coach and Horses, standing by itself at the junction of Holborn Street. Currently closed. The pub, located on Liverpool's ridge, apparently had tunnels which led down to the nearby former Bridewell on Prescot Street. The site is probably of ancient date and was formerly a coaching house and site of a turnpike for the old stage-coaches travelling in and out of Liverpool during the 19th century.

The pub was named the Low Hill Coffee House pre-1880s and was a noted political house in the 1840s. At that time, land west of Hall Lane was in use as a cricket ground, whose team used the pub as their headquarters. Whilst east of Hall Lane the land was used as a parade ground for military purposes until 1870s/1880s when terraced property swamped the area.

Cricket, like tennis, was associated with the upper classes in the 19th and early 20th centuries. Yet the game of cricket has always been played in the streets of towns and cities across the country. As many readers will recall, the wicket would either be a lamp post, or chalked onto a brick wall. Few working-class lads, if any, would have become first-class cricketers. An old story tells of a group of lads from an inner city school, who were taken for a day out over to the Wirral. Finding a clearing in the woods, the teacher suggested they have a game of cricket.

"How can we play, Sir?" one of the lads asked, quite innocently. "There's no lamp post."

The barriers of snobbery diminished as the 20th century progressed. Yet even up to the early 1960s, cricketers were still referred to as 'gentlemen and players', and the MCC, for example, only allowed women members into their realm in 1998.

The following extract from 1888 concerns cricket at Hall Lane:

'The Roscoe was probably the best and most noted club that played in Hall Lane and it always put a first rate eleven in the field. I think the Roscoe was originally started in connection with a social club of the same name, which had a short and unsuccessful existence in Bold Street in 1847. The Roscoe cricketers at once established their headquarters at the old 'snuggery' in Low Hill and continued to hold their club meetings, annual dinners and match suppers there until the club and its members were played out. The club had the audacity to challenge the Famous All England Eleven to play twenty-two of its members and, the local team gave Old Clarke's 'half a score and one', a most emphatic 'licking'.

The Roscoe players were assisted by four members of the Bootle Club but the current jelly swells of the Liverpool, which then had its own very select and exclusive ground in Wavertree Lane, scornfully refused to take a hand in the game.

Those current jelly snobs of the Liverpool (their survivors, if any are left, must be 'potent, grave, reverend seigneurs') always held themselves snobbishly aloof from the other local clubs and they only condescended to play once a year with the aristocratic I Zingari Club*. Several lords were usually included in the gypsy eleven and that was why the Liverpool Lord Lovers challenged the lords and always got beaten.

Cricket is first recorded in Liverpool, as being played 'about' Cazneau Street, before 1800. Soon after, a number of clubs were formed in various parts of the town.

The Liverpool in question, played at a ground adjacent to Spekeland Cottages, south of Wavertree Road, near Edge Hill Railway Station, both since demolished. The current Liverpool Cricket Club was established at Aigburth in 1881.'

*I Zingari means gypsy, or wanderer and the word is more well-known locally nowadays as an amateur soccer league.

The Raven

The Raven was formerly listed at the junction of Low Hill and Phythian Street. In this late 1960s photograph, the two shops were occupied by Miss A Taylor, Newsagent at 38 and E Beveridge Ltd, Typewriter Dealers at 36. The pub was demolished in the early 1980s to make way for road improvements.

Swan Hotel

The Swan Hotel was situated at the corner of Low Hill and Meaburn Street, whose former three storey houses are featured in this early 1960s photograph. The adjoining shop, number 45, was listed to S Gordon & Co Ltd, Grocers. Both the site of the pub and Meaburn Street are now an industrial estate. Listed 1970.

Another of the streets off Low Hill is Low Wood Street (originally Wood Street East), which presently contains housing from the 1960s, 1970s and 1990s.

This view is from a bygone age, clearly showing a court, Kensington Place, adjoining the pub. Washing is hanging out on the line, with another court, Mornington Terrace, on the left. Nine courts and five pubs were crammed into this street. The faded name of the pub is displayed over the window, and it was compulsorily purchased in 1905. Photograph from the 1890s when managed by Richard Healey.

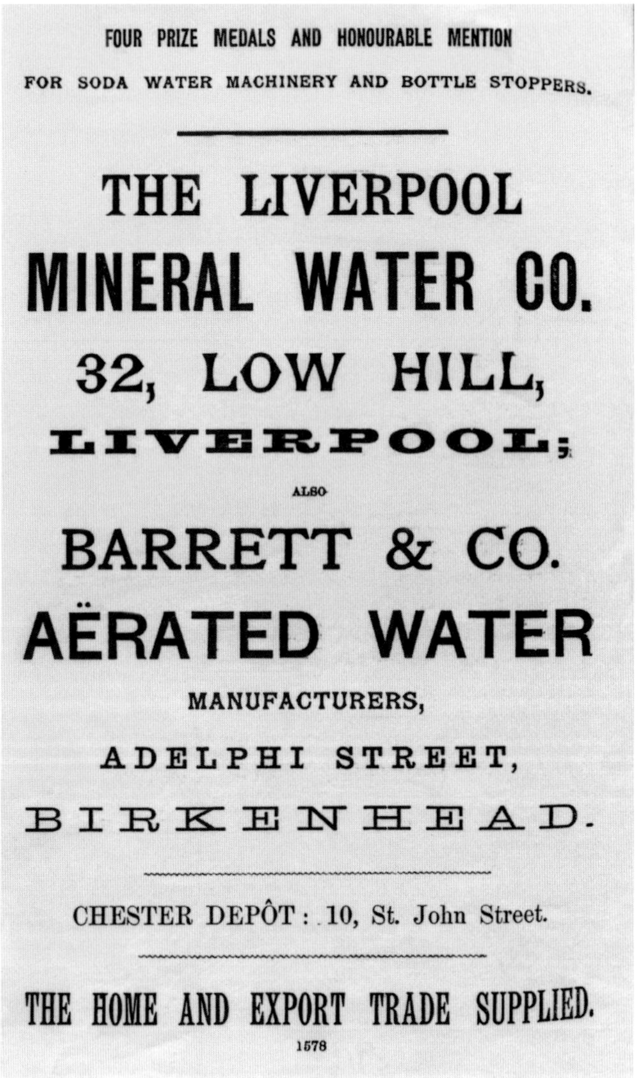

Beer House

Prior to the 1970s, a myriad of crowded streets stood in this vicinity. This pub was located at 120 Phythian Street, off Low Hill, one of ten formerly in the street. Named the Crown Vaults before closure in the 1920s, the premises was then listed to a Confectioner. The photograph above, is from approximately 1900, when Mary A Johnson managed the pub.
Police Report 1903: Quoits and dominoes played here.

Old House at Home

This advertisement for the Liverpool Mineral Water Company, formerly 32 Low Hill, is from the 1890s. By the 1920s, the premises was listed to a Furniture Dealer.

Walker Street still leads off West Derby Road. Prior to the 1970s a number of small streets led from Walker Street to Baker Street, one being Mela Street, now abolished, on whose junction this pub was located.

Listed at 41 Walker Street, and one of four original pubs, it was a Beer House when this view was taken in 1912. The manager at this time was Thomas Formby. From the late 1930s, this pub was named the Lord Raglan. Listed 1964.
Police Report 1892: Domino playing allowed in this house.

The following two, from an original four pubs, were in Penton Street.

Penton Arms

Listed at 45 Penton Street and 108 Farnworth Street, the premises was listed as a Beer House and Brewer before the 1880s. The mass demolition that occurred off both sides of West Derby Road in the 1960s and 70s cleared numerous terraced streets, including Penton Street. Marion Williams was licensee when this view was taken in the 1960s. Listed 1970.

The Cottage
Formerly listed at 4 Hutchinson Street, which stood between Baker Street and Upper Baker Street, the Cottage closed in the 1920s, and modern housing now occupies the site. Photograph from the 1890s when Jane Taylor managed the pub.
Police Report 1892: Tip-it playing allowed in this house.

The Lord Raglan

Waterloo Hotel

Located at the area where Penton Street continued across Farnworth Street, at the junction of Empire Street, now abolished. Displaying its name on the window and managed by Thomas Quinn when this picture was taken in the 1920s. Listed 1970.
Police Report 1892: Quoits and domino playing allowed.

Farnworth Street, which was originally Kilshaw Street South was renamed after John Farnworth, Mayor, in 1865, and had seven pubs along its length. Number 45, a private house, was listed to Albert Gray, Secretary of the Royal Antediluvian Order of Buffaloes, known as the Buffs, a friendly society, from the 1930s to the 1950s. Although the society had some premises of its own, pubs were frequently used for meetings.

The initials were displayed on a number of pubs all over the town, two being featured in this publication: the Clarence and the Cumberland, both in Everton Road.

Boaler Street remains as a thoroughfare in this vicinity, where the following two pubs, from an original five, are located.

Cumberland Arms

Known locally as the Flower House and located on the corner of Goldsmith Street and Boaler Street, this pub is open to date. The view is from the 1920s when the manager was Thomas Waterworth Gibbons. The adjoining sweetshop, which in the 1920s was listed to Robert Hands, Confectioner, still trades today.

Newsham Park Hotel

Open to date at 108 Boaler Street, at the junction with Butler Street and known locally as Mac's. This photograph shows how the pub looked in the 1920s, when the manager was Robert Gawthorne.

The exterior differs today with the side door, next to the shop, closed up and one of the side doors in Butler Street also gone. The adjoining shop, which belonged to Copes Tobacconist and Newsagent, has since been demolished, with the site now landscaped. Butler Street is displayed on the glass of the gas-lamp.

Pub names throughout the country are as numerous as they are variable, most originating from religious, royal, or heraldic names, or famous people. In Liverpool, as elsewhere, many naval heroes have been honoured in this way. Yet, somewhat strangely, only one pub commemorates one of our greatest military and naval commanders – Sir Walter Raleigh (142-144 Boaler Street).

Great Homer Street

The following pubs, covering the remainder of Everton, are, with a few exceptions, all in Liverpool 5.

Below the gracious mansions and villas of the Everton slope, a narrow thoroughfare, named Homer Street and Boundary Road, ran northward from Fox Street, parallel with Scotland Road.

The rapid rise and spread of the population began to encroach beyond the boundary of Liverpool and Everton in the 1830s, as the Everton township was absorbed into Liverpool. At this time, Homer Street and Boundary Road were both widened and renamed Great Homer Street.

By the mid-19th century, the merchants had moved on to new districts, as seemingly endless terraced streets gradually wiped away all traces of the gentry east of Great Homer Street.

The street soon became established, with its well-known market, numerous shops, pubs, pawnbrokers etc, all still within the living memory of the local population.

Also associated with 'Greaty', as it is affectionately referred to, were the many 'Mary Ellens' who lived in the teeming streets that lined either side of Great Homer Street, when it became the most densely-populated area of the city. This was a name given to women who worked, mainly on barrows, in this area, generally selling flowers and fruit and vegetables in all weathers. It was a very hard life and produced a special breed of women whose distinguishing attire was a shawl, worn winter and summer.

The 1960s sounded the death knell for the old Greaty, although the market still trades on Saturdays. However, gone are the numerous terraced streets and, rather unusual for a main thoroughfare, not one its nearly 40 original pubs remains.

Times have certainly changed along Greaty since the mass demolition and only one modern pub currently trades – the Lamplighter (see the Seven Stars, Gordon Street, page 118).

Many of the old communities of Liverpool, particularly during the 1960s, were scattered far and wide as the bulldozer raised their homes and local corner pubs to oblivion.

This area was known for its particularly close-knit communities. Memories still linger on of course, although fewer and fewer people now recall pre-war Greaty.

Older relatives and friends of mine can recall just a few of the memories of Great Homer Street: the smoking of clay pipes that filled the air in the pubs with thick smoke, popping into the pub for a swift rum at 6 o'clock in the morning on the way to work and moneylenders having the best 'spec' in the pub, as they sat distributing the money.

The shops sold everything, always at low prices. And, on a Saturday night, at the end of trading, often after midnight, a scramble for the Sunday joint would frequently occur, when people who had bided their time, often acquired their meat free.

East Side

The following pubs were on Great Homer Street.

Box House

Listed at 34 Great Homer Street and situated close to Sheridan Street, this pub was named the Spread Eagle before the 1880s. When photographed in 1905, when the manager was James Thomas Elliott, a Barber Shop adjoined the premises. Not listed 1930s. Landscaping now replaces this block.
Police Report 1903: Selling drink to a drunken man, dismissed.

The Elephant

This huge, flamboyant structure was situated at 56a Great Homer Street and 2 Roscommon Street. In the 1920s, when this view was taken, the Elephant was managed by Daniel Kelly. The site is now landscaped. Listed 1964.
Police Report 1903: The bar is divided into two compartments without internal communication outside the counter. Selling drink to a drunken man, dismissed.

Clock Vaults

The Clock Vaults formerly stood at 76 Great Homer Street at the junction of Back Roscommon Street (abolished). This view, taken before the First World War, features the pub's clock and a barefoot child happily playing in the gutter, next to the adjoining Blackledge's shop. The manager at this time was John Elliott. Not listed 1940s.

Oporto Vault

Situated at 124 Great Homer Street at the junction of Arkwright Street (originally Earl Street), this pub was managed by John Lewis when photographed in the 1920s. The old terraced houses of this street have now been replaced with landscaping, although a few modern houses have been built on the top of Arkwright Street during the 1990s, where it is now realigned. Listed 1964.
Police Report 1900: Selling drink to a drunken man, dismissed.

Swan Vaults

Located at the corner of Conway Street, at 152 Great Homer Street, this photograph shows the pub, prior to demolition in the 1960s. The manageress was Dorothy Blanche Wilson and the premises was locally known as Gertie's. Listed 1970. The adjoining shop was occupied by CE Jones, Butcher. Conway Street is abolished at Great Homer Street, with a section higher up the slope remaining devoid of all the old property. The pub's nickname reminded me of another Gertie, not a pub, but a mechanical substitute to replace barmaids in the 1960s. The tub-shaped dispensers enabled customers to purchase their beer by dropping money into a slot machine on the bar. This, the first experiment of its type in the country, occurred in the Grapes, Whitechapel, in the city centre. Needless to say, the customers did not approve of the machines and the barmaids soon returned.

The pub was also one of the first in the country to experiment with metric measurements. The premises has since been demolished. Somewhat ironically, the site of this former pub is now part of the major regeneration of the former Queen Square/Whitechapel area and, from being a former commonly-named corner local, the site is now a massive pub with a typical 1990s name – the Rat and Parrot.

Foresters Arms

172-174 Great Homer Street, at the corner of Elias Street, now abolished. The adjoining shop was the British Empire Meat Co when photographed in the 1920s and the manager was Thomas O'Donoghue. Note the group of Mary Ellens outside the pub, listed 1964.

The Buckingham

Situated at 188-190 Great Homer Street, at the corner of Buckingham Street, with a Cocoa Rooms next door. A horse is just visible in the side street in this shot, taken around 1908, when the manager was Benjamin Lock. Not listed 1940s. The street still remains, although now realigned at the edge of a sports centre.
Police Report 1892: Supplying drink to a drunken woman, 20/- and costs. Conviction quashed by recorder on appeal.

At 58 Buckingham Street was a pub named the Buckingham Palace – doubtless not quite on a par with its London namesake! Premises listed as the Star Social Club just before World War 2.

Jamaica Vaults

On the same block as the former, but at 198 Great Homer Street, on the corner of Howe Street (abolished), this pub was named the City of New York Hotel before the 1890s. The adjoining shop, Dennisons, was a Grocers and Provisions Merchants. The site is now part of Everton Sports Centre. When photographed in the 1920s, the manager was Jeremiah O'Donoghue. Listed 1964.

Edinburgh Castle

Another Great Homer Street pub, at 206, at the corner of Edinburgh Street (abolished). Here, the pub can be seen shortly before its demolition in the 1960s, when the licensee was Shelagh Margaret Conlan. Listed 1964. The two adjoining shops, closed and awaiting the bulldozer, were Perry & Roulston, Grocers and Norman's Footwear Stores.
Police Report 1900: Selling drink to a drunken man, dismissed.

Mediterranean Vaults

This pub, at 214 Great Homer Street, at the junction of Luther Street (abolished), is now part of Everton Park. The manager was Arthur Matthew Mitchell. The adjoining Draper's Shop belonged to Sidney Green. Not listed 1940s.
Police Report 1892: Permitting drunkenness, dismissed.

The Peacock

Listed at 238 Great Homer Street where it joins Anderson Street. In this 1960s shot, when the licensee was Eileen Dutton, the premises is seen standing in isolation. The street still remains, skirting Everton Sports Centre. The pub displayed a date of 1854 and was known locally as the Anderson. Listed 1970.
Police Report 1982: Supplying drink to a drunken man, dismissed. Supplying drink to a girl under 14 years, dismissed.

Sefton Arms

Situated at the corner of Thomaston Street at 258 Great Homer Street, next door was the British Wallpaper Stores. Photographed in the 1920s when the manager was William Wilson. Not listed 1940s.

Thomaston Street

Although no longer on its original line, Thomaston Street still stands and contains housing built in the 1970s to replace the old terraced property.

An all too familiar scene of present day Everton, the remaining property of Thomaston Street, now realigned, is undergoing the final stages of demolition, surrounded by housing built in 1999/2000.

West Side

New Market Inn

At the corner of Juvenal Street, at 1-3 Great Homer Street, in front of the North Wholesale Fruit, Vegetable and Hay Market, which opened in 1841, and stood between Great Homer Street, Juvenal Street, Cazneau Street and Great Nelson Street. In this early 1960s photograph, a lorry loaded with potatoes can be seen leaving the market. The pub's manager at this time was Patrick Molloy. Listed 1964, the site now partly surrounds the Kingsway Mersey Tunnel. Note the 'Great Homer Street' name-plate dangling precariously, as the adjoining premises had just been demolished.

Old Market Inn

Adjoining the former premises, at number 5 Great Homer Street. Both pubs were named after the old market that stood behind this block. Photographed in 1912 when the manager was Joseph Holbart. Although demolished in the 1960s, the pub ceased trading in the 1920s and became the Liverpool Fruiterers Association Ltd.

In 1867, a special licence was granted to this and a number of other pubs of the vicinity, to be kept open for the accommodation of persons attending the North Haymarket, between 2pm and 4am on Wednesdays and Saturdays. Although intended for farmers and other people on business at the market, no doubt locals would have swelled the custom and many a brawl would have occurred on Saturday nights/Sunday mornings while the licence was in force. The special licence was withdrawn in the 1870s.

Houghton Arms

This large public house, at 7 Great Homer Street and 83 Great Nelson Street, is typical of the late 19th century structures that were frequently erected on street corners as the city expanded. Pre-1890s, it was called the Squire Houghton Vaults and, from approximately 1890 to the First World War, it was also listed as the Liverpool District Farmers' Club. The manager was Henry Jones when this photograph was taken in 1912. The premises was named after a former mansion built early in the 19th century by Edward Houghton on the site of the pub. Listed 1964.
Police Report 1902: Permitting drunkenness, dismissed.

Carnarvon Castle

Listed at 31 Great Homer Street where it joins Collingwood Street (abolished). The sign saying 'To Public Baths', refers to the former Burroughs Gardens Baths. Photographed in the early 1960s when the manager was John Davies. Listed 1964. The adjoining shops were Mrs Rose, General Dealer at number 33, Magnet Supply Stores (Liverpool Ltd), Grocers & Provision Dealer at 35-37, J Pegram Co, Tea Merchants at 39 and M Wilson, Draper at 41.

Crown

Although this pub, at 45 Great Homer Street, at the corner of Virgil Street, is now long demolished. The street survived the mass clearances that occurred in this vicinity to make way for the second Mersey Tunnel. Clearly displayed in this 1960s view are two shops: Maurice Wilson at 41 and W Costigan at 43, where one of their lorries is making a delivery. Listed 1964.

Dryden Arms

This former Bent's house, listed at 77a Great Homer Street and 80 Dryden Street, was photographed in the 1960s as a barrow woman prepares to set out her fruit and vegetables on the corner. Listed 1964. The adjoining shops were: JJ Hewlett, Butchers at number 77, Milwyn Evans, Boot and Shoe Dealer at 75 and FJ Waterson, Baker at 73.
Police Report 1902: Selling drink to a drunken man, 20/- and costs.

Newsham House

This pub, at 167 Great Homer Street, at the end of Newsham Street, was known locally as the Little Newsham, probably to distinguish it from the other Newsham House, which was at the other end of Newsham Street, on the corner of Scotland Road. This photograph is from the 1920s, when the manager was Edward Charles Thomas. Not listed 1940s.

Homer Vaults

Located at 199 Great Homer Street, at the junction of William Moult Street (shortened), is this ornate, highly-decorated pub, the Homer Vaults. When photographed, in approximately 1912, it displayed the manager's name as John Voge, together with an advertisement for 'Rare Old Rums' over the door in William Moult Street. Some barefoot children are standing outside the adjoining Drapers Shop, belonging to Jacob Abrahams. Not listed 1940s. The site now forms the outer perimeter of an industrial estate.

Clock Vaults and Derby Arms

The top view, from the 1960s, features the Clock Vaults, listed at 213 Great Homer Street at the junction of Louis Street (abolished) and the Derby Arms, at the junction of Taylor Street (shortened). At this time, Ann Dowd was manageress of the Clock Vaults and Rosaline Grace Kay of the Derby Arms, which, pre-1890s, was called the Machine Vaults. The three shops which separate the two pubs were: The Clock Café, Robert Armstrong, Grocer, and Bill's Market, Fruiterer. Both pubs listed 1970.

In this second view, from 1912, the Clock Vaults can be seen in more detail and features two Mary Ellens, selling what appears to be bundles of secondhand clothes, stacked unappealingly in the gutter. The manager at this time was William James.

Homer Cinema

A former cinema of Great Homer Street, located between Kew Street and Bostock Street. In common with the majority of suburban cinemas, the late 1950s and 1960s was the end of an era for the affectionately nicknamed 'flicks' or 'flea pits'. This particular one closed in 1962.

The following were located in the former crowded streets east of Fox Street/Great Homer Street.

Beer House

Located at 117a Upper Beau Street (shortened) off Fox Street, at the junction of Garden Lane, with the name of the street displayed on the gas-lamp. The premises closed in approximately 1912 and the site is presently landscaped. Photographed in the 1890s, when the manager was Charles Jackson.
Police Report 1892: Selling beer and rum to a girl under 14 years, dismissed.

Talbot Arms

Listed at 49 Prince Edwin Street, at the corner of Beresford Street, the Talbot Arms was one of eight former pubs on the street. When photographed in approximately 1900, John Murch was manager. Listed 1970. Modern housing now occupies this site.
Police Report 1892: Selling drink to a drunken man, 4/6 and costs. 1903: The back kitchen window of the adjoining shop looks into the yard of the licensed premises.

The following extract is from 1912:

'The Prince Edwin Street area contains approximately 187 houses, of which 163 are insanitary. The area is situated in a congested district and the site of the houses in Ebor Street, although small in extent, would provide a much-needed open space, to be used as a recreation ground. The total population is 825 and the average death-rate, per thousand, per annum for the six years 1905 to 1910 is 38.78.'

Prince Edwin Street

This photograph was taken approximately 1912. An old boarded up Beer House is featured at the junction of Beresford Street (opposite corner to the previous pub). It would appear that the property was about to be demolished, as the pawn shop in the centre of the block was advertising that the business was to be transferred. The property higher up the street was fronting courts.

The Fleece

This pub was formerly situated off Prince Edwin Street, at the junction of Clifton Street (abolished) and Giles Street (only 29 yards long). The street sign indicates 'Giles Street, late Short Street'. Since this was obviously an appropriate name, I wonder why it changed? When photographed in the 1890s, the pub was called the Fleece but it had previously been known as the Lamb and in this view it displays the name, Mulchrones, (see next picture). After closing in the early 1930s, the premises was converted to stables. Nowadays it is part of a modern structure – Campion High School for Boys.

This picture is of Michael Mulchrone, taken at the wedding of his eldest daughter, Annie, together with the best man, Scotty Cooper, in 1917. Annie Mulcrone, (note the spelling of her surname) married Harry Anders, who became the chief chef at the Tudor Restaurant in Lewis's Department Store, Ranelagh Street, Liverpool during the 1930s.

Michael Mulchrone was a well-known Liverpool Victualler from the 1890s to the First World War. Originating from County Mayo in Ireland, he married his wife Mary at the RC Pro-Cathedral of St Nicholas in Liverpool in the 1880s.

Together with many of his fellow countrymen, he came to Liverpool at a time of widespread poverty in the town, although money was there to be made for those with the determination. After first living in Collingwood Street, off Scotland Road, he rapidly acquired a number of pubs and eventually moved to Walton Park, off Rice Lane, which in those days was on the outskirts of town (see the Maid of Erin, Athol Street, page 66).

The following pubs, all in the Everton and Scotland Road areas, were also owned by Michael Mulchrone.

The Elephant	56a Great Homer Street and 2 Roscommon Street (page 105).
Dryden Arms	78-80 Dryden Street and 77a Great Homer Street (page 109)
The Shrewsbury	183 Richmond Row.
Beer House	81 Opie Street (page 117).
Athol Arms	14 Athol Street (page 68).
Maid of Erin	37 Athol Street (page 66).
Spirit Vaults	108 - 110 Boundary Street.
Beer House	16 Eldon Street.
Beer House	53 Skirving Street.

Listed to his wife Mary were the following two pubs.

| Richmond Vaults | 80 Gregson Street |
| Green Flag | 130 Vauxhall Road (featured in Volume 3) |

As explained in Volume 1, after 1904 numerous pubs were forced to close. This affected Michael Mulchrone along with many others and he diversified into Greengrocery and Fish and Chip businesses. The pub at 80 Gregson Street, for example, was listed as a Greengrocers by 1912. Ill health forced him to retire to 40 Spencer Street, Everton, where he died in 1918. His wife resided at this address until her death in the 1950s.

The Beresford

Before the 1970s, Beresford Street was amongst the former maze of streets, running from Cornwall Street to Bute Street (now realigned and shortened). The Beresford was one of five former pubs on the street and was situated at the junction of Upper Beau Street. In the 1920s, at the time of this shot, when managed by George Cameron, the pub was a typical, bare-looking local, displaying no lettering, except on the windows. Listed 1964.

Foresters Arms

Also situated amongst the teeming network of streets that once covered the area, the Foresters Arms was located at number 1 Thorncliff Street (abolished) where it joins China Street.

This picture is from the 1920s when the pub was managed by Mrs Jean Hamilton. The premises was converted into the Thorncliff Social Club in the 1930s.

Police Report 1903: Domino and quoit playing allowed in this house.

Beer House

This old Beer House, was located in China Street (abolished), which once ran from Beresford Street up to Netherfield Road South. Originally one of two pubs, the premises was compulsorily purchased as long ago as 1906. Photographed in the 1890s when the licensee was Sarah Melbourne.

The following three pubs, from an original eight, were in Roscommon Street.

Farmers Arms

This pub at 18 Roscommon Street, was originally a private house, built around 1820, when the wealthy merchants of Liverpool began to escape the crowded town by moving out to the Everton slope. During the 1860s it became a Public House, and from the 1870s until sold, the premises was run by the same family – the Senars. This photograph was taken in the 1960s when the manageress was Margaret Blanch Bridges.

One family member, Edwin James Senar (Ted), actually ran the pub from 1891 until his death in 1947. His son, Thomas Edwin Senar, was also associated with the pub, mainly involved in the bottling and delivery side of the business. He was born on the premises in 1893 and worked there until his retirement in 1948, when the pub was sold to the Tetley Walker Brewery.

Incidentally, the pub was still lit entirely by gaslight until sold. It was demolished in the early 1980s.

The large dwelling houses at 20 and 22, adjacent to the premises, were converted to the Roscommon Music Hall in 1892. Then, in 1911, they became a Picture House, the Roscommon Picture Palace, renamed the Roscommon Cinema (known as the Rossie) in 1940, which closed in 1958.

Unusually, for what was, after all, only a side street, another picture house, the Tivoli, stood here and closed in 1954.

Police Report, 1892: Back door opens into a large stable yard in which there are three stables, a joiners shop, and a house. The stables and shop are sub-let and the house is occupied by a man in the employ of the licensee. The police have access at any time through a side gate.

The Senar family, well-known in the licensed trade, was involved in various pubs, including the following, which were either owned, tenanted, or managed by different members of the family, at various dates throughout the 19th and 20th centuries.

Unlike Michael Mulchrone's pubs, the following were spread throughout the city:

ABC Vaults	4 Jackson Street, Liverpool 8.
Aigburth Hotel	26 Aigburth Road, Liverpool 19 (see Volume 2).
Beer House	21 Smithdown Lane, Liverpool 7.
Coach and Horses	27 Woolton Street, Liverpool 25 (see Volume 2)
The Cottage	104 Devon Street, Liverpool 3.
The Crown	41-43 Lime Street, Liverpool 1 (see Volume1).
Farmers Arms	Frankby, Wirral.
The Garrick	19 Great Charlotte Street, Liverpool 1 (see Volume 1).
Kings Arms	32 Islington, Liverpool 3 (page 44).
King Harry	55 Blessington Road and 56 Anfield Road, Liverpool 4 (featured).
Little Woodman	3-5 Hill Street Liverpool 8 (see Volume 2).
North Star	189a Great Homer Street and 75 Bostock Street, Liverpool 5.
Old Swan	possibly the Original Old Swan Liverpool 13.
Rigby's	23-25 Dale Street, Liverpool 2 (see Volume 1)
The Savoy	29 Lime Street, Liverpool 1 (see Volume 1).
The Vines	87 Lime Street, Liverpool 1 (see Volume 1)
Wine & Spirit Vaults	128 Limekiln Lane, Liverpool 5 (see Volume 3).

The two labels are evidence of bottling activities at the Farmers Arms from the 1880s period, when the licensee was Thomas Senar. The bottling was done by hand, each bottle held under the tap of the cask. This laborious task involved the operator being exposed to the fumes for a considerable number of hours, more often than not ending up intoxicated, without a drop passing his lips! I wonder how many applications for the job would be received if such a trade was advertised to-day!

Featuring labels from the inter-War years. The Guinness was brought over from Dublin to bonded stores in Liverpool, in ships owned by Guinness. After being brought to the cellars of the Farmers Arms, the product would be bottled and labelled ready for sale.

Wynstay Arms

Built on the corner of Roscommon Street and Portland Place, this pub was called the Wynstay Arms in the 1880s, prior to being named the Orangeman's Arms. This title related to the fact that the area was a stronghold of the Orange Lodge Order and remained so until the mass demolition of the 1960s. For a short spell prior to demolition, in an unsuccessful effort to stay open, it was renamed the Cotton Picker. This view is from the early 1980s, when it stood closed, awaiting demolition.

Royal Arms Vaults

Listed at 123 Roscommon Street, at the junction of Abram Street. Pre-1890s it was a Spirit Vaults. Photographed in 1908 featuring the manager's name as James Parle. On the gable-end is R Parles – Branch, not listed 1930s.

When the house which was to become the Farmers Arms was built, Roscommon Street was almost totally rural. The street has almost reverted to its original state, and is currently barren of any buildings being used as a thoroughfare through Everton Park.

Incidentally, Sir Herbert Morton Stanley (1841-1904), British explorer of Welsh birth, resided for a time at 22 Roscommon Street. He was sent by Gordon Bennett, proprietor of the New York Herald, to find the Scottish Missionary, David Livingstone (1813-73), in Africa. His ultimate meeting with him was reputedly marked by his famous greeting, "Doctor Livingstone, I presume?"

Beer House

Formerly listed at 17 Mellor Street (abolished), where it meets Arkwright Street, a little further north than the previous street. This photograph is from the 1920s, when the licensee was John Howard. By the 1930s the premises was no longer a Beer House, and had been taken over by a Fried Fish Dealer.

Police Report 1903: Selling drink to a drunken man, dismissed. Domino playing allowed in this house.

The following two pubs were in Opie Street (abolished, originally Duke Street).

Opie Street Vaults

As can be seen in this 1908 view, the Opie Street Vaults, which was listed at number 28, was just a terraced house that had been converted into a Beer House. A seemingly homemade sign was placed over the window. The premises lost its licence in 1913, when the licensee was Annie J Black.
Police Reports 1902: Selling drink to a boy under 14, bound over. 1903: Quoits played here. Trade entrances; one in Opie Street, one in passage between Opie Street and Arkwright Street.

Beer House

Formerly Listed at 81 Opie Street. This picture, taken in 1903, when managed by Emanuel Rodick, features quite a crowd of onlookers. This premises also lost its licence in 1913.
Police Report 1902: Selling drink to a drunken man, dismissed; Entrances, one in Opie Street, one in passage between Opie Street and Beatrice Street.

Gordon Arms

Located at the corner of Gordon Street and McGill Street (both abolished), the Gordon Arms was one of three former pubs situated here that have since been replaced by modern shops and open grassland. Photographed in 1908 when managed by Joseph Edwin Lowe. Listed 1964.
Police Report 1903: Selling beer to a boy under 14 years, bound over.

Seven Stars

As featured, numerous pubs were located in this vicinity before the 1970s, but this pub, located in Gordon Street, was one of only five comparatively modern ones. This view was taken in 1972. After long periods of closure, it was finally demolished in 2000.

The other four modern pubs were, or are:
The Lamplighter	Great Homer Street, open to date.
The Tugboat	Netherfield Road North, open to date (see the King Edward Hotel, page 119).
The New York,	Netherfield Road North, currently closed.
The Jester,	Jason Street, now converted to a funeral parlour.

Edinburgh Vaults

The Edinburgh Vaults, at 65 Edinburgh Street (abolished), was one of three former pubs of this street. The writing over the windows and on the lamp of this old pub indicates Barker's Huyton Ales. When photographed in 1908, the manager was William Milligan. By the 1930s, the premises was listed to a Shopkeeper.
Police Report 1892: Selling drink to a drunken man, 4/6 +costs.

Beer House

Another of the former crowded streets off Great Homer Street was Aughton Street (abolished) where this old Beer House was listed at number 60. Its licence expired in the 1890s and it was named the Old Ship before closure and conversion to a shop. This picture was taken in the 1890s when managed by Sarah Watson.
Police Report 1892: Card and domino playing allowed.

Parallel with Great Homer Street, but situated higher up the Everton Ridge, is Netherfield Road, both North and South, which was originally a narrow country lane called Netherfield Lane.

As the mansions which once graced the vicinity were swept away, the unpretentious terraced streets took over. Pubs, shops, and houses soon spread at an alarming rate along its frontage during the last century and it eventually boasted a total of twenty-four public houses.

Today, this previously densely-congested road has turned full circle and it now runs through Everton Park, with very little old property remaining.

Netherfield Road South in the 1920s

Photographed from the corner of Prince Edwin Street, just visible to the right of the picture is one of the three brass balls hanging on the pawn shop, which belonged to Hugh Jones.

The main building was a former Boy's Industrial School. Beyond the school, at the junction with Brow Side, is the Ann Fowler Salvation Army Memorial Home for Women, originally opened in 1867 as a Welsh Independent Chapel. This building, despite its listed status, was demolished in the 1980s. The site is now part of Everton Park.

The following two premises were on Netherfield Road South.

Atlantic Vaults

Situated at 61 Netherfield Road South where it meets China Street. This view was taken shortly before the pub's demolition in the 1970s, when the manager was Richard Kelley.

The Queens Arms

The Queens Arms once stood at the junction Netherfield Road South, at number 75, and Cornwall Street (abolished). Both the pub and the high-rise flats in the background (Garibaldi House), have been cleared since this photograph was taken in the 1970s.

The following were in Netherfield Road North.

West Side

King Edward Hotel

Located at 1-3 Netherfield Road North, on the corner of Abram Street and displaying the name McLachlan's, after the licensee, Mrs Elizabeth McLachlan, who was the manageress when this 1908 photograph was taken.

King Edward Hotel
This modern shot shows the previous pub empty and awaiting demolition in the 1970s, with a new pub, the Tugboat, open to date, in the background. The 1970s-built dwellings on the left were demolished in the early 1990s.

The Vale

Formerly listed at 51 Netherfield Road North, at the junction of Rose Vale, this pub was listed as a Beer House before the first World War and photographed in the 1920s when the manager was Henry H Thomas. Premises closed approximately 1960.

The Grapes

Situated at 165 Netherfield Road North at the corner of Howe Street, the Grapes' manager was Robert Scaife when photographed in 1908. Listed 1964. The adjoining shop was listed to Daniel Higgins, Butcher.
Police Report 1892: Serving a drunken man and permitting drunkenness (2 informations), dismissed.

The Albion

Standing at the junction of Edinburgh Street, with old property still standing on the steep hill, this former Bent's house, at 173 Netherfield Road North was photographed in the 1960s, when managed by John W Cumper. Multi-storey flats now occupy the land behind this and the next pub. Listed 1964.

The Game Cock

A Beer House pre-1880s. Photographed in the 1890s, when the manager was Frederick Clarke and the premises was listed at 185 Netherfield Road North, on the corner of Ellison Street. This view shows a General Dealer at 187, once part of the pub and next door, landing houses. Premises listed as the Devonshire Social Club just before WW2. strangely, in an 1892 Police Book it was the only Liverpool pub in which draughts were allowed.
Police Report 1892: Selling drink to a drunken woman, 10/ and costs. Draught playing allowed in this house.

East Side

This 1920s view of Netherfield Road North shows abundant landing houses and terraced properties on the steep Everton Ridge. The site is now part of Everton Park.

Pre-War tenants would not have had an inkling that from the 1950s and more particularly the 1960s, their streets would have been replaced by huge, high-rise flats. The city faced a formidable housing problem after the Second World War in which 6,585 houses and flats had been totally destroyed and 125,310 dwellings damaged. The problem was exacerbated by demobilisation and a shortage of both labour and materials.

One of the earliest schemes to combat the chronic shortage was the prefabricated dwelling or 'prefab'. Between 1945 and 1947, 'temporary' prefabs were installed on 40 sites around the city. Although initially built on a short term basis, many survived until the 1960s.

However, this was only the tip of the iceberg and, mainly due to the chronic shortage of land, in the early 1950s, consideration was given to the construction of high-rise flats. In 1953, the year of the Queen's Coronation, the foundation stone for the first block was laid in Sparrow Hall, about a mile from the city boundary, aptly-named Coronation Court.

Although the first to be started, for various reasons it was not finished on time and Cresswell Mount, at the top of St George's Hill, Everton, became the first multi-storey block to be completed and tenanted, with building starting in 1954 and the block being opened in 1956.

Since its completion, the number of blocks to follow was phenomenal. By 1965, seventy-nine blocks had been constructed, not only in the city, but also in the outskirts such as Kirkby, Huyton and Halewood, with a further twenty-nine under construction, ranging from ten to twenty-two storeys in height. 'What goes up must come down', is an old saying and, remarkably, the high-rises began to 'tumble down' after less than thirty years. Many have been, or are due to be demolished.

Cresswell Mount

This view of the Cresswell Mount block was taken during demolition in 1984 (see Everton Terrace).

Stanley Arms

One of only five pubs that stood on the eastern side of the road, the Stanley Arms was listed at 318, at the junction with Adelaide Street. Note the large advert for Cains Old Rums. This picture dates from 1908 when the manager was Albert Turner. Pre-1880s it was named the Royal Standard. Just before the outbreak of the Second World War, the premises was converted to the First Liverpool (Lord Mayor's Own) Group Boy Scouts Headquarters.

Two pubs of Netherfield Road North were the Monarch of the Glen at 143 and Threlfall's Public House at 183, both listed 1964. Two unique names of Netherfield Road South were the Prince Charlie Public House, on the corner of Prince Edwin Street and Emillie St Pierre, on the corner of Upper Beau Street, both listed 1964. The latter was named after a ship.

During the American Civil War, William Wilson was Captain of the Emillie St Pierre. Whilst endeavouring to run a blockade into Charleston, South Carolina, he was intercepted and captured by a federal war steamer, the James Adger.

Wilson, his cook, and a steward, were retained on the ship as it headed to Philadelphia. On the third day, amazingly and heroically, Wilson and his two companions somehow recaptured the ship, clapping their captors in irons, then they sailed, unaided, across the Atlantic, where, with colours flying, they arrived in the River Mersey on the morning of 21 April 1862.

Needless to say, Wilson and his two companions were hailed as heroes and were richly rewarded. The owners of the ship paid the cook and steward £300 each.

The steward, John Penny, opened the pub with his reward, naming it after the ship. Some reports claim that he was not actually a steward, but the ship's carpenter and that his axe, which he used in recapturing the ship, was displayed in the pub for a number of years.

Returning to the pub itself – with such a name, it is of no surprise that a nickname would be in order from the locals and the pub was long known as Cheesmans, after a former manager, Leonard Cecil Cheesman.

The following pubs were situated on the Everton slope.

Prince Rupert

Listed at 2 Rupert Lane (abolished) and 1 Village Street (Village Street was in Liverpool 6), also having an entrance in Brow Side. This pub was named after Prince Rupert, who used a cottage facing as his headquarters in 1644, during his siege of Liverpool during the Civil War (see Everton Terrace, page 125).

Just north of the pub stood a large house and grounds, built in 1790, named Rupert House. After its demolition, the site was used as a military ground and barracks, finally becoming a recreation ground.

The pub itself was so named from the 1890s, prior to which it was known as the Everton Coffee House, one of the oldest pubs in Everton. It was a noted political house during the 19th century, when the manager was a well-known victualler of his day – Ned Halliday.

The pre-First World War photograph above, shows the gable-end of the pub with 'Established 1644' written on it. The manager at this time was William Denovan. I am inclined to think this referred to the siege of that year, rather than the pub being established. It is recorded that the premises was licensed by 1770. Listed 1970.

When the pub's manager, Bill Denovan (Senior), was married, he celebrated the occasion at the pub. Being an Everton supporter he invited all Everton's pre-War team as guests. Coincidentally, a friend of mine, John Wheatland, also an avid Evertonian, recalls celebrating his evening wedding reception at the pub in 1956 – obviously a 'true Blue' pub.

Close to this pub, at 22 Village Street, stood the Queen's Head Hotel, which closed in the 1890s. This was the venue for a meeting which took place in November 1879 to discuss a new name for the St Domingo Football Club which had been formed the previous year. They adopted the name Everton Football Club, after the district.

The players during those early days were mainly attached to the church, but such was the rising popularity of football and so many were involved in it who were from outside the church, that the name was changed. The team played in Stanley Park at the time and, by 1880, Everton was admitted as a member of the Lancashire Football Association.

Another meeting took place in the Sandon Hotel, Oakfield Road, Anfield, in 1882. This resulted in the team moving to a field off Priory Road the following year. Relocating once again, in 1884, to a field off Anfield Road, the Sandon Hotel, managed by John Houlding, was adopted as the club's headquarters. The club won its first trophy this year – the Liverpool Cup.

The team became one of twelve founder members of the Football League in 1888. Although the ground was suitable at Anfield, internal disputes, mainly over the rent charged by John Houlding, led rivals including a George Mahon and his supporters, to leave Anfield and move across Stanley Park for the 1892-93 season, into a new, purpose-built stadium, Goodison Park, the first major ground in the country, (Celtic Park, Glasgow, was inaugurated at the same time as Goodison Park). After moving, a new team took over at Anfield – Liverpool Football Club (see Albert Public House, page 142).

William Ralph (Dixie) Dean

Numerous players have graced Goodison Park since the 1892-93 season and, of course, many books have been written on Everton Football Club. I will briefly mention just one player, arguably the greatest goalscorer to grace English football, and undeniably the greatest Everton player of all time – the immortal William Ralph Dean. Amongst his many achievements is his record of scoring 349 League goals in 431 games, including 34 hat-tricks (36 in all matches). Remarkably, his record of scoring 60 League goals in one season, 1927-28, still stands to-day.

Everton Football Club itself also has a unique record. Since the inauguration of the Football League in 1888, it has been in the 1st Division (Premier League since 1992) longer than any other team and has amassed more points and scored more League goals. This remarkable record still stands in the year 2001. Sadly, for a team of Everton's sporting history, the 1990s saw a never-ending struggle to stay in the top flight.

Ironically, just over 100 years after moving from Anfield to Goodison Park, another debate between fans has been an impending move to a new stadium.

It was an enterprising move from Anfield over a century ago and, into a new millennium, another bold move does seem to be on the horizon. Into the year 2001, a site at King's Dock on the waterfront appears to be the preferred location for a move away from Goodison Park.

A tradition of the club is the distribution of Everton Toffee at home games. This originated with a Molly Bushell, born about 1736, whose toffee is said to have been taken from a recipe belonging to a Doctor Gerrard and which brought fame to the Everton district. Royalty enjoyed Everton Toffee as the following advert shows from the time the business was run by Molly's grandson: 'Estd 1753. As supplied to HM The Queen and HRH The Duke of Cambridge, Lord John Russell etc and manufactured by RH Wignall, grandson to Molly Bushell.'

This sandstone structure, built in 1787, was a former 'lock up', still seen today on the green above Shaw Street. Located right in the heart of the original Everton village, unsurprisingly, Everton Football Club adopted the structure into its present badge.
This 1936 advertisement, showing two boys wondering who Everton were going to play, concerns a dispute between the pools companies, hence no opposition is featured.

Football pools became popular in the 1920s and, in February 1936, the Football League withheld the fixtures until the last moment, hoping to force the pools out of business. But the opposite happened, throwing the game into turmoil and the dispute only lasted for three weeks. The public was 'hooked' and the pools went from strength to strength.

The following two pubs, from an original six, were in Everton Terrace (originally Middle Lane).

Beer House

Located on the corner of the steep Copeland Street at the corner of Everton Terrace, the premises was, during the 1860s, named the Purple Vaults and, by the 1880s, the Cambrian. Photographed as long ago as the 1890s, when managed by Michael Murphy. Not listed 1912.

Beer House

Another old Beer House listed at 51 Everton Terrace. Adjoining the pub stood court property, Listed at number 3 court when photographed in the 1890s, when managed by Thomas G Hughes. The premises was compulsorily purchased in 1912. The court property in Everton Terrace, was the limit of such property eastward. From here onwards, up and over the ridge, the area became built up with the more familiar terraced property.

This view of a former police station at 33-35 Everton Terrace, was photographed during the early 1960s. It was then owned by the Liverpool City Police, a substation of Prescot Street Police-Station, in the old B Division. Opening in 1925 as Everton Police Station, this building had previously been the Liverpool Certified Industrial School. Mr S Robinson was listed as the last governor, with Mrs Grace W Robinson the last matron. It closed in approximately 1922. By 1930 it was listed as Recruiting and Training Department and, from 1940, Everton Police Station and Stores. The force amalgamated with Bootle Police in 1967, becoming Merseyside Police in 1974. The structure was demolished in the early 1970s.

The closed-up building facing the station, probably a former Stables, was on a part of the former land belonging to Rupert House. The block of multi-storey flats beyond, is Cresswell Mount.

One of the pubs of Everton Terrace, on the junction with Brow Side, aptly-named the Artillery Vaults, was built on the site of an old cottage used by Prince Rupert during the siege of Liverpool in 1644. The cottage must have been of ancient date as, prior to it being demolished in 1845, it was apparently in danger of falling down. Its old timbers were used to make souvenirs, including knife handles, ornaments, frames etc.

The following extract, written in 1887, shows that, even in those days, the City Fathers often showed little respect for buildings of historical interest:

'While his troops encamped on Netherfield Common, Prince Rupert's cottage remained standing until the present century, when it was sold and pulled down for the benefit of thirsty people, a gin palace being erected on its site. It is to be regretted, but it is a fact, that Liverpudlians, as a body, have no respect for historical relics, the old castle and the old tower, as well as this cottage, have given way to modern vandalism and other ancient landmarks have followed suit, wherefore Liverpool now wears the aspect of an entirely modern town.'

St George's Hotel

The steep St George's Hill used to lead to Northumberland Terrace from Netherfield Road North. This pub was located on St George's Hill, junction of McGregor Street. After the demolition of the street, the frontage of the former McGregor Street became the site of St George's Heights in 1966. This huge, twenty-two storey block dominated the Everton sky-line until it too 'tumbled down' in the year 2000. Photographed in 1912, when the manager was Henry J Henshell.

Beer House

A former Beer House, situated amongst the once-congested streets that lined the Everton slope, was photographed in the 1890s when managed by Jane Powell. This extremely small pub was situated at 24 York Terrace, where it joined Dukes Road. It is surprising that this road was even named, as it was only an alley some 68 yards long leading from York Terrace alongside the edge of a former school – Our Lady Immaculate, to Patmos Street. The premises lost its licence in 1904 and was named the Duke of York before closure.

Northumberland

One of two former pubs on Northumberland Terrace, this one, at 121, was situated at the corner of Bethesda Street, a very steep street, which was only 47 yards long and led down to Cicero Terrace. It was a typical family house, known locally as Graham's. Photographed in approximately 1960, when it was managed by Ellen (Elsie) Ryan. Listed 1964.

Liverpool, of late, has established itself as a venue for film-making. During the 1960s, when films were rarely made here, this pub was used for a TV documentary about a Former Everton Football Club legend, Alex Young, named 'The Golden Vision', a nick-name given to him by the fans.

Albion Hotel

Parallel with Northumberland Terrace is Albion Street. This former Beer House, listed at number 62, was photographed in approximately 1903 when the licensee was Elizabeth Keddie. The premises closed in the 1920s, although the old housing of the street survived until demolition in the 1970s.

In the late 18th and early 19th centuries, the mansions of Everton extended to a little beyond Church Street (later Heyworth Street), at the summit of the Everton slope and St Domingo Lane (later St Domingo Road), on the verge of the slope. One writer of the time described the vicinity as follows:

'The splendid old stone houses rising one above the other, as on the sea-front at Genoa, were surrounded by ample gardens and approached from their gates by winding terraces picturesquely cut in the rocky foundation.'

One such house was built near the summit around 1770 by William Clarke, a well-known Liverpool banker of his day. During 1806 it became the property of Nicholas Waterhouse, an eminent member of the Society of Friends. After enlarging the house, a passage which ran between the mansion wall and the kitchen garden, was named Waterhouse Lane. Michael James Whitty, Liverpool's first Head Constable later occupied the house.

Riots between the 'Orange and Green' were commonplace in Liverpool in the 19th century and one particularly nasty riot occurred in 1835, involving Mr Whitty, reported by J A Picton, of which the following is an extract:

'On July 12 a repetition took place, with more than usual violence, of the disgraceful scenes called 'Orange Riots' in which two Irish factions dispute the palm for distinction in ferocity and brutality. The anniversary of the Battle of the Boyne occurred on a Sunday. It was expected that a grand demonstration would be made by the Orangemen; but if such was intended, it was prevented by the occurrences which took place. Collections of the lower classes of the Irish assembled in the streets of the North end of the town; and about ten at night a fracas took place in Ben Johnson Street, which led to the capture of one of the ringleaders by the police. This was the signal for a general row. The mob set upon the watchmen, rescued the prisoner and assaulted the officers so hotly that they were driven from the street. Another commotion arose in Great Crosshall Street; and the two mobs uniting, being fifty to one as compared with the officers, the latter were compelled to take flight and seek refuge in the lock up in Vauxhall Road. This the rioters proceeded to break open with axes and staves, with loud cheers and outcries from an assembled crowd. Those inside, barricaded the inner doors and retreated to the loft, where they rang the alarm fire-bell. Mr Whitty, the head of the night police, hearing the bell, drove at once to the station, where he was attacked with the utmost violence. Being a powerful man, he contended boldly with his assailants; but it might have gone hard with him had it not been for two young men amongst the rioters who gallantly espoused his cause, and assisted him to dash through the door which had just been broken open. The rioters then paused, as if uncertain what to do next; and assistance having in the meantime arrived, the mob were gradually forced back and, in their turn, compelled to fly.'

The riots resumed on the following day in Park Lane, south of the city centre and Vauxhall Road, north of the city centre. A similar situation then occurred, with the following, the rest of Picton's writing:

'Many of the rioters were taken into custody, on whom were found pistols, with powder and ball, and other deadly weapons. The most active of them were tried and punished.'

The following year a new police force was introduced to the town, with the consolidation of the day, night and dock police as one body, a system originally introduced by Sir Robert Peel into the Metropolitan Police. Mr Michael James Whitty, previously Superintendent of the Night Watch, was appointed Head Constable. Almost twenty years later, Mr Whitty was the founder of the regional morning paper *The Daily Post*, in 1855. Mr Whitty had a daughter, May, who was born in Liverpool in 1865 and, after a distinguished stage career, she was made a Dame Commander in 1918, later settling in Hollywood where she began making films. Her most famous part was probably that of the vanishing lady in Hitchcock's *The Lady Vanishes*. She died in 1948.

By the mid-19th century, the old house itself, in common with neighbouring mansions on the Everton slope, was raised to the ground to make way for the ever-advancing terraced properties which swamped leafy Waterhouse Lane, (see Thistle Public House). Pubs galore were built as part of this process to accommodate the expanding population and, unlike the older pubs nearer the city centre, these new pubs were mainly named.

Over the last three decades, the whole area has changed once again. The terraced streets and numerous pubs have been obliterated and Everton Park now occupies a large area. When Church Street was renamed Heyworth Street, after James Heyworth, a former landowner of the vicinity, fifteen pubs lined this main thoroughfare. The number is currently down to three.

The following were, or are, on Heyworth Street.

West Side

Heyworth Hotel

This pub, at number 11, was situated at the corner of Kepler Street (originally Christian Street North). During the mass demolition from the 1960s, this pub was apparently earmarked to be spared the bulldozer. However, in the confusion of the demolition process, it was pulled down instead of the Thistle, which somehow survived demolition.

Looking at the architecture of the pub, it is a mystery why it was demolished along with the whole west side of Heyworth Street (except the Thistle). The manager during the 1960s, when this picture was taken, was George H Roberts. Listed 1970.

Thistle

Open to date at 33 Heyworth Street, it is the only old structure still left standing on the west side of the road. This picture was taken in the 1960s, when managed by Mrs Mary J Hardman. Located at the junction of the former Waterhouse Street (originally Waterhouse Lane, abolished except for a few yards alongside the pub) and named the Thistle when it was built around 1876. Prior to this date, another pub named the Wheatsheaf stood on this site. The premises currently displays a nickname, The Little House on the Prairie, because it now stands in isolation at the edge of Everton Park.

The Elephant

Located at 59 Heyworth Street and 57 Stonewall Street (abolished), now part of Everton Park. This shot is from the 1960s, when managed by Margaret Hannah. Listed 1964. The premises next door was listed to Mrs D Lund, Shopkeeper.

Raven

This pub, at the corner of Cochrane Street, at number 93 (originally Canning Street), had previously been a Wine and Spirit Vaults and earlier, before the street changed its name in the 1870s, was called the Canning Vaults. Surprisingly, a tiny section of this street still remains in Everton Park where a chapel still stands. Photographed in approximately 1960, when the manager was William Alfred Spiers. Listed 1964.

The Priory

A former Higsons' House, on the corner of Priory Road (abolished), at 145-147 Heyworth Street, the premises was a Beer House before the 1880s. For many years the premises was known locally as Fred's Cozy Corner, but this was gradually replaced by another nickname, Lulu's. Listed 1970. Photographed in the 1960s, when managed by Frederick J Waller. The adjoining shop belonged to Mrs E Williams, Greengrocer.

Priory Hotel

Listed at 159-161 Heyworth Street, a little northward from the last featured pub, stood a former Bent's house, also called The Priory, quite justifiably, as it stood at the junction with Priory Mount (abolished). Until approximately 1905, it was named the Heyworth Hotel. George Alfred Green was the manager when this picture was taken in the 1960s. The pub was known locally simply as the Priory. The adjoining shop was listed to James Roberts, Pet Food Stores. Listed 1964

Police Report 1900: Selling drink to a drunken man, dismissed.

St George

Listed at 195 Heyworth Street (originally at 29 Church Street, when it was the first pub of the vicinity). Formerly close to St Georges Church, a modern School, replacing an earlier one, now occupies this site. Photographed in the 1960s when managed by George William Goodwin, by whose surname the pub was known. The adjoining premises was listed to Frederick Clark and Sons Ltd, Builders, (see Mere Bank Public House). Listed 1970.

East Side

London Stores

A former Threlfall's house at 2-4 Heyworth Street at the junction of Breck Road. Few people knew this pub by its correct name and always referred to it simply as the London. This photograph was taken during the 1960s, when managed by Phyllis Hewitt. Pre-1880s it was called the Illuminated Clock. The adjoining shop was listed to James Maxwell, Newsagent.

Garrick

Formerly to be found at 64 Heyworth Street on the corner of Lance Street. This picture was taken in the 1960s, when managed by Lily Connor. Wong's Fish Bar can be seen next door. Listed 1970. The site is now landscaped, fronting modern housing facing Everton Park.

The Old Campfield

Open to date at 98 Heyworth Street (132 when opened in the 1860s), at the junction with Hamilton Road. A former Bent's house when photographed in the 1960s, when managed by John Bird. Currently standing in isolation, it may have been named after the former barracks in nearby Rupert Lane, which had opened in 1848.

Paganini Hotel

Listed at 172-174 Heyworth Street, this pub was situated almost opposite the St George, at the junction of Church Place. The picture above is from approximately 1880, when managed by Alexander Thomson.

Various members of the same family ran the pub from the 1830s until approximately 1880, when the address was also listed as a brewery. The same family had involvements with the facing St George at various dates during the same periods.

It was reputed that the famous Italian violinist, Nicolo Paganini (1784-1840), stayed at the inn whilst on a visit to Liverpool, hence its name. Paganini was in Liverpool in 1832 and performed six concerts in the old Theatre Royal. There was widespread discontent at the high prices charged for his concerts, the cheapest seats costing five shillings in the gallery, well beyond most people's pockets. He tried to make amends by giving his services free at a concert for the relief of the poor.

Paganini Hotel

Featuring the previous inn's replacement, built after 1880, then at 162 Heyworth Street. I was informed that before demolition the pub had an engraving of the original inn on one of its windows. The smaller section on the right of this photograph may have survived from the original, after extensive alterations.
Photographed approximately 1960, when the manager was Clifford Samuel Johnson. Listed 1970.
Police Report 1900: Selling drink to a drunken man, bound over.

Mere Bank

Open to date at 178 Heyworth Street and 1 Mere Lane and named after Mere Bank House, which existed in a triangular setting between Mere Lane, Beacon Lane, and Breckfield Road North in the mid-19th century. The Mere Bank is a highly-decorative pub, displaying the date 1881 on its frontage. Amongst the alterations that have occurred since this photograph from the mid-1960s, when managed by Eleanor Pearson, is the conversion of its corner window into a door. The library on the extreme left is the only other structure still standing. The shops were Bill's Hairstylist, at 176, Mrs R Johnston, Fruit Shop, at 174 and Mrs W Wibberley, Butcher, at 172. The man by the pick-up may have worked for Frederick Clark and Sons Ltd, Builders, outside whose premises the photograph was taken. The pub may have been rebuilt in 1881. Prior to this date a pub of the same name was listed, although addressed at number 2 rather than 1 Mere Lane.

The continuation of Heyworth Street is St Domingo Road, where the following pub, originally one of four, is located.

Valley Hotel

Open to date and situated at the junction with Everton Valley, this flamboyant structure was known as the Gardeners Arms pre-1870s, then the Prince of Wales until the 1890s. Before renovation, the bar inside the premises was on a steep incline, handy for anyone wanting to seem taller! The photograph dates from the 1920s when the manager was William Herbert Glover. The adjoining shop, originally part of the pub, was listed to William Allen, Piano Dealer.

In 1968, this pub was under a compulsory purchase order and in grave danger of being bulldozed. By 1970, at a meeting of the Corporation's Housing Committee, it came to light that the Corporation had an agreement with the Liverpool and District Brewers Association, to safeguard as many pubs as possible in areas of redevelopment. After various discussions between the interested parties, the compulsory purchase order was finally lifted. Local pubs are still closing some thirty years later, but for different reasons, such as dwindling trade and changing drinking habits. This pub has closed and reopened a number of times of late and is currently open.

The following were situated east of Heyworth Street, the first two were in Hamilton Road.

Hamilton Arms

Photographed in 1912, when the manager was John A Field. Located at 43 Hamilton Road where it meets Downing Street, which used to lead into Hamilton Road from Breckfield Road North. The street still remains, although now realigned, containing modern housing. In common with various pubs of similar shape, the premises was nicknamed the Flat Iron. Not listed 1940s.

The Primrose

This pub, on the corner of Minor Street (abolished), was called the Yorkshire Arms pre-1890s. This view features the former terraced housing of Hamilton Road which was demolished, along with the pub, in the early 1980s. Modern housing now lines Hamilton Road.
Police Report 1903: Selling drink to a drunken man, dismissed.

The following two were, or are, in Rishton Street (abolished).

Chalk Farm

This unusually-named pub stood at the junction of Rishton Street and Poplar Street, so named since the 1860s. A former Bent's house, managed by Frederick Thomas when photographed around 1960. Modern housing now occupies this site. Listed 1970.

Breckfield

Open to date at 133 Rishton Street. The houses just visible in the street have long been demolished and, although since the clearances the street no longer exists, the pub is still addressed in Rishton Street. With the realignment of the modern property, nearby, Rishton Close retains the name of the original street. This view is from the 1960s, when it was an Ind Coope house managed by William A Freeman. The pub has since been renamed Turpin's.

Red Lion

Pre-1880s it was named the Lion Inn, formerly at 4 Rendal Street, at the junction of Poplar Street. Managed during the early 1960s by Patricia Griffiths when this shot was taken. Listed 1964.

Ancient Briton

Listed at 32 Mere Lane where it joins Ermine Street. Neat bungalows now stand on Ermine Close, replacing the old terraced housing of Ermine Street. Managed by Zillah Thomas when photographed during the 1960s. Listed 1970.

The following four, from an original seven, were or are on Breckfield Road North (formerly Hangfield Lane) a main road of Everton which, pre-1970s, led through to Beacon Lane. From Mere Lane, a section of the road has since been swallowed up by a housing estate. At this point, its continuation becomes Robson Street.

Beer House

Open to date at 18 Breckfield Road North and named the Royal Arch Vaults, pre 1890s, then listed as a Beer House until after the First World War, when it became known as the Theatre Vaults, probably after the nearby Theatre Royal on Breck Road. In line with the modern trend, the pub has reverted to its former nickname of the Hole in the Wall.

The photograph shows the premises when it was still a Beer House, in approximately 1908, and managed by Thomas Munro. On the window is written Kops Ale and Stout. A company, Kops Ale, was registered as having stables between Shaw Street and Haig Street in 1901, whilst Kops Ale itself, was one of the first low alcohol beers, brewed towards the end of the 19th century.

Thirlmere

This large corner local at the end of Thirlmere Road, was open for business when destroyed by fire in 1994. This view shows the premises shortly afterwards, before demolition. The site is currently open land.
Police Report 1900: Unjust measure in his possession, 10/- and 7/6 costs.

The Rutland

This pre-First World War Beer House was situated at the junction of Rutland Street (abolished). Photographed in the 1960s, when the manager was Robert Cardwell, the pub was demolished in the early 1980s, with modern housing now occupying this site. The adjoining shop at number 85, was Dean's Fruit Stores.
Police Report 1903: The grocery business formerly carried on at this shop has been discontinued and nothing but drink is now sold.

St Domingo

This pub was situated on the corner of Breckfield Road North and Towson Street, in a section of the road that has been replaced by the Grisedale Housing Estate. Threlfall's houses rarely displayed their names and this pub is no exception, as can be seen in this 1960s view, when the manager was Thomas Melling. Listed 1970.

The continuation of Breckfield Road North is now Robson Street, originally containing four pubs, including the following two.

Cumberland Hotel

A former Mellors' house at 33 Robson Street and 19 Towson Street, this pub was named the Old Stingo, pre-1880s. After demolition in the 1970s, the site became part of the new Grisedale Estate. The premises was known locally as Ted Baker's, after a former manager.

A Typical Everton Scene

The section of Towson Street which led from Robson Street to Breckfield Road North was known locally as Little Towson Street before the new estate was built, with the rest of Towson Street to Walton Breck Road remaining, but now physically split up.

The Park at number 183, one of two other pubs listed in Towson Street, still remains, facing Liverpool's football ground. A date of 1888 is displayed, indicating that the pub must have been re-built, as a pub was listed on the site in 1871.

The typical Everton scene above shows a section of the Grisedale Estate on Robson Street, about the site of the Cumberland, during demolition in 1998, just over twenty years after being built.

This sad state of affairs still persists in the city and it is somewhat ironic that as comparatively modern housing continues to be demolished, numerous terraced houses, built over 100 years ago, still remain in abundance.

The Liver

Formerly at 129 Robson Street, on the corner of Beacon Lane, this pub was photographed in the 1960s, when the manager was Ronald Jones. The premises was known locally as Fitzy's, after a former manager, Frederick Fitzgerald. Listed 1970.

The following three pubs, from an original six, were in Beacon Lane, realigned and greatly reduced in length.

Beacon Light

A small corner local that stood midway along Beacon Lane, listed at 80 Beacon Lane and 43 Wye Street (realigned). This picture is from the 1960s, when the manager was Francis Henry Wilson. The former municipal flats, Sir Thomas White Gardens, faced the pub, which survived until the 1980s, before succumbing to the bulldozer. Listed 1970.

Alexandra

Situated at 134 Beacon Lane, at the junction of Breckfield Road North (to the left). Photographed in the 1960s, when managed by Edward Ellis, the site is now part of the Grisedale Estate. Listed 1970.

The Brighton

Located at 178 Beacon Lane, on the corner of Jeffery Street (abolished, originally Brighton Street, hence the pub's name), which led through to Robson Street pre-1970s. Photographed approximately 1960, when managed by Mrs Elsie Smith. Listed 1970.

Breck Road (originally Breck Lane) was once a country lane which led through countryside to Clubmoor and Norris Green, now a main road of Everton, with one side Liverpool 5, the other Liverpool 6.

Between Heyworth Street and Breckfield Road North, all the frontage on its north side was cleared during the 1970s, whilst the other side has also since been cleared as far as Breckfield Road South. The road originally contained fourteen pubs.

The following were, or are, on Breck Road.

North Side

Kings Arms

Listed at number 87 Breck Road, where it meets Creswick Street (abolished). Photographed in the 1920s when the manager was Joseph Miller, the two shops adjoining were Augustus J Stephens, Tailor at 89 and Mrs Cecilia Colleti, Florist, at 91. Listed 1970.

Police Report 1892: Quoits played here and supplying drink to a drunken man, 10/- and costs.

Castle

This pub was listed at 123 Breck Road and 1-3 Tynemouth Street (abolished). The pub displayed a date of 1882. Paul Michael Baxter was manager when this shot was taken around 1960. The area was cleared in the early 1970s and is currently landscaped.

Tynemouth Street was the location of John Houlding's Brewery until just before the Second World War, when taken over by Ind Coope. He was manager of the Sandon Hotel at the time of the split, when Everton Football Club left Anfield.

The Crown

This pub at 227 Breck Road, on the corner of Fowler Street, is in a section that still retains its old structures, between Breckfield Road North and Oakfield Road. This early photograph is from the 1890s, when managed by Elliot Morley. The pub ceased trading in the late 1960s, and is currently an Estate Agents.

Breck Road House

Open to date at 263 Breck Road, on the corner of Breck Road and Rydal Street, the pub was known as the Richmond Hotel up until the First World War. This view is from the 1920s, when it was the Breck Road House and the licensee Edward H Willis. Note the three doors in use on Breck Road, with one in Rydal Street. Only one door is currently in use on Breck Road and one in Rydal Street. The landlord reinstated the name Richmond just before the Second World War. In 1982 the pub changed names once more, to the Lutine Bell and for many years was known as Goodwins.

The Britannia

This pub at 283 Breck Road, on the corner of Coniston Street, ceased trading in the 1980s and is currently used for a different business. The manager when photographed during the 1960s was Wilfred Callaghan.

The Breck

Located at the corner of Windermere Street, at 297 Breck Road, the Breck is open to date. In this 1890s view, when managed by James Buckler, four doors were in use, currently there is just one.
Police Report 1892: The licensee is a traveller in the employ of the owners, and does not appear to take any part in the management of the business.

South Side

The Campfield

This large corner pub at 70 Breck Road and 1 MacKenzie Street (abolished) was called the Everton Hotel pre-1880s. It was demolished in the late 1960s and the site landscaped. Managed by Herbert Wardle when this view was taken in the 1960s.

At the junction of Breckfield Road South, at 154 Breck Road, this pub is open to date. This view is from the 1960s when it was a Bent's house managed by John Hogg. The Theatre Royal next door, which opened in 1888, became the Royal Cinema in 1920, until its closure in 1965. It then became a Bingo Hall and is currently a Furniture store. The pub, which was built before the theatre, was called the Museum Hotel in the 1860s and, by 1880, the Royal Museum Hotel. Then the word 'museum' was dropped from the sign to give the pub its current name.

Police Report 1892: Back door opens into enclosed passage between licensed premises and the music hall next door, thus making a means of communication to the latter place, which could be used if desired. The back door of the public house is kept locked.

Mona Castle Hotel

George and Dragon

Listed at 118 Breck Road and 65 Newlands Street (abolished). Named the Bull and Mouth pre-First World War, then the George and Dragon when photographed in the 1920s, when the licensee was Thomas Formby. After the War, it was renamed the Commercial. Listed 1964. The site is now landscaped.

Police Report 1903: Domino playing allowed in this house.

The Royal Hotel

Located at 250-252 Breck Road at the junction of Woodville Terrace, this former Greenhall Whitley pub was named the Mona Hotel pre-1890s. The pub was demolished in the early 1980s and the site is now modern housing, fronted by a landscaped area. Managed in the 1960s by Frank Coole Faragher.

Police Report 1892: Summoned for keeping open during prohibited hours, dismissed.

The following two pubs are in Breck Road, Anfield, Liverpool 4 and the remainder are also in Liverpool 4.

The reason that this section of the thoroughfare is so named, is because originally it was situated outside the municipal boundary.

The junction of Breck Road/Oakfield Road westward, was Everton (Liverpool 5), whilst eastward it came under Walton-on-the-Hill. When Walton was absorbed into Liverpool, this became part of the Anfield area (Liverpool 4).

The numbering, somewhat strangely, is still opposite to

Liverpool's, where the numbers radiate outwards from the Town Hall.

The three pubs on this section (continuing westward along Breck Road) are therefore listed – The George at 124, Richmond Arms 78 and the Cabbage Hall at 20.

Richmond Arms

Open to date at the junction of Breck Road and Westcott Street, the shops that now adjoin the pub were not even built when in this 1890s photograph, when managed by Maurice Archdeacon. They were constructed in the early 20th century and are shown in the 1970s view below.

Cabbage Hall Inn

A drawing of the original pub from 1862, where the manager's name, Turner (Jesse), is displayed over the door. This was demolished in the 1930s and replaced by the present structure.

The gable-end of the adjoining houses shown on this view, still stand on Breck Road today and are currently in use as a Builders' Merchants.

There are a number of theories concerning the unusual name of this pub, including the following three:

i. Jesse Turner named it after his practice of growing huge cabbages on adjoining land and was reputed to have had a cabbage stalk nearly eight foot long hanging in the pub.
ii. A local greengrocer had a huge house built in the vicinity, so pretentious by local standards that it rapidly acquired the nickname, Cabbage Hall.
iii. A mansion built hereabouts had stone pineapples built on the gateposts and local children, not knowing what they were, called them cabbages, hence the name.

Personally, I think it may be one of the last two, as the Cabbage Hall was listed in the 1820s, some years before Jesse Turner became the manager.

Police Report 1902: Licensed for music and singing. Room on ground floor.

he following two of three pubs are in Anfield Road (originally Anfield Lane).

King Harry

This pub, at the corner of Anfield Road and Blessington Road, is currently closed and looks almost the same today as it did in this 1920s shot, when managed by Thomas Crook. The main feature is the corner door, which has now been converted into a window. The pub displays a plaque, stating a building date of 1885.

Living in Blessington Road during the 1960s, this was one of the first pubs I frequented. A well-run family house, it was managed by Hughie Donnelly for nearly 20 years until 1982.

Breckside House Hotel

Situated at 336 Anfield Road and 377 Walton Breck Road, this pub is open to date. The first photograph dates from 1905, when David Sutherland managed the pub. Note the old triangular school sign on the gaslight and what appears to be an eagle at the top of the pub, removed on the later view.

The above photograph is from the 1960s, when George Parsons was the manager and a large concrete lamp standard had replaced the old gaslight. In common with other, similarly-shaped pubs, it was known as the 'Flat Iron' and this has now been adopted as its name.

The site of the remaining pub, the Arkles, earlier the Royal, at the junction of Anfield Road and Arkles Lane, was in the north-east corner of a large area called Ann Field (hence the name of the district) on a map of 1768.

On an 1830s map, structures such as Anfield House and Anfield Villa are named. These have since been replaced by a number of terraced streets. Anfield Cottage, located near Priory Road, has also been replaced by houses and Anfield Lodge has been replaced by Anfield Road School.

The following three pubs are on Walton Breck Road.

Stanley Hotel

Standing at the corner of Walton Breck Road and Beacon Lane (realigned), the Stanley is open to date. The gargoyles over the main entrance on this view, from approximately 1970, when managed by Jimmy Peters, still remain, although the former Off Licence has gone. Known locally as the Bent's, after the former Bent's Brewers, the premises displays a date of 1891.

Police Report 1892: A staircase has been built from the second storey of the licensed premises into a large enclosed yard at the rear, which is used by Bent's Brewery Co as a bottling store, and is said to be used for domestic purposes only.

Salisbury Hotel

Open to date at the junction of Burnand Street, this distinguished-looking pub, typical of the late 19th century, opened in 1884. Photographed in 1998, when the licensee was Shelagh Griffith.

It was named after the Marquis of Salisbury, Robert Arthur Talbot Gascoyne Cecil, 3rd Marquis of Salisbury (1830-1903), British Conservative statesman. He succeeded Benjamin Disraeli, 1st Earl of Beaconsfield, as leader of the Conservative Party in 1881 and subsequently headed three governments (1885-1886, 1886-1892 and 1895–1902).

The political scene of the late 19th century is now part of history and few, if any, residents of the terraced streets around the pub will be remotely aware of the fact that their streets are named after men who shaped modern history.

The Marquis of Salisbury's nephew, Arthur James Balfour, was Prime Minister from 1902-1905. His name is commemorated in Balfour Street, almost facing the pub.

Adjoining Balfour Street is Gorst Street, named after Sir John Gorst, Parliamentary Secretary at the time of an Education Act, which became the foundation of the Education system in England and Wales.

Adjoining Gorst Street is Randolph Street, named after Lord Randolph Churchill, whose son, Sir Winston Leonard Spencer Churchill, statesman (1874-1965), held the following positions: Under Secretary of State for the Colonies, 1906-1908, President of the Board of Trade, 1908-1910, Home Secretary, 1910-1911, First Lord of the Admiralty, 1911-1915, Secretary of State for War, 1918-1921 and for the Colonies, 1921-1922, Chancellor of the Exchequer, 1924-1929 and Prime Minister, 1940-1945, 1951-1955.

Facing the Pub stand Burleigh Road North and South, both named after Burleigh, the seat of the Balfour family in Scotland.

Behind Burleigh Road North is Goschen Street, named after Lord Goschen, who succeeded Lord Randolph at the Exchequer.

The Salisbury family owned extensive tracts of land in and around Liverpool and, prior to the mid-19th century, facing the site of this pub, on what would become Burleigh Road North and South, the land was listed to Mary Salisbury.

Albert

The Albert is open to date and listed at 183 Walton Breck Road. This picture was taken in the 1970s, when the manager was Robert Dawson. The pub was known locally as Cassidy's for many years.

However, the main feature of this view is the former Spion Kop of Liverpool Football Club, adjoining the pub (see Everton).

The Kop was named after a hill near Ladysmith, South Africa, the scene of a battle in January 1900, during the Boer War, when the British were defeated, with the loss of 322 lives and over 500 wounded.

The name was adopted about 1906 in memory of the tragic defeat. Although the name was not only confined to Liverpool's ground, it became affectionately associated with the club.

The Kop was extended and covered in 1928 but sadly for thousands of 'Kopites', it had to be demolished after the Taylor Report recommended that all Premier League grounds had to be seated.

The previous photograph, from the 1950s, shows the other end of the Kop with the gable-end of the Albert just showing beyond the ground. The old admission prices are clearly displayed as 1/9d (approximately 8p) in the Kop and 4/6d (approximately 22p) in the stand.

The Kop was demolished in 1994, then rebuilt, and despite other major improvements to the ground, somewhat ironically, into the year 2001, Liverpool FC, like Everton FC, are contemplating relocating to a different site. At the time of writing, the club have not discussed any particular site, although it seems they may opt to stay in Anfield.

Returning to the Cabbage Hall vicinity, an almost triangular green space still exists at the junctions of Walton Breck Road, Breck Road, Priory Road and Lower Breck Road. Also, an old marker from 1817 still remains by a former street tap of 1856.

This is an ancient site and originally two of the narrow country lanes, Townsend Lane and Lower Breck Road, led out to the then distant West Derby Village, the first through Clubmoor and Norris Green and the other through Tuebrook.

As noted elsewhere, many seemingly modern pubs, are rebuilt over older structures in former rural areas.

Two early Townsend Lane pubs are the Clubmoor and the Farmers' Arms, both in existence prior to the 1860s when they served a rural community, whilst two later pubs of the thoroughfare derive their names from former farmhouses – Elm House and Willow Bank House.

The Clubmoor was originally the Tichborne Arms pre-1880, possibly named after a controversial trial of the time, involving Sir Roger Tichborne, heir to a Hampshire baronetcy, who disappeared in a shipwreck in 1854.

In 1865 a man in Wagga Wagga, Australia, announced that he was the missing baronet, and came to England to pursue his claim. After a notoriously long trial, the man was found to be Arthur Orton, son of a London butcher and he was subsequently sentenced to fourteen years penal servitude.

Despite being named the Clubmoor for over a hundred years, the pub is still referred to as the 'Titch' by some regulars.

The following three pubs, from an original five, are in West Derby Village, Liverpool 12.

This village shop at number 1, long known as Cooper's Corner, has traded since the 1950s and is still an Off Licence. Few people will now remember that prior to the 1950s the premises was a Beer House.

Hare and Hounds

Despite now being part of the city, West Derby village still retains its old village identity. There has probably been an inn at this location for centuries when the surrounding farming communities would have gathered for social events, particularly since West Derby was historically such an important township.

This view is from the 1890s when the licensee was Charles Candeland. Since this photograph, was taken, the building has undergone extensive exterior alterations. Next to the pub stood the Liverpool United Tramway & Omnibus Co Ltd and is now modern shops.

The registered owner in 1892 was Thomas Baxter, a Brewer, who must have been fond of the name of his pub, as he also acquired the Prince Albert Vaults at 6 Commutation Row in the city centre, which he changed to the Hare and Hounds.

West Derby Public House

This tranquil village scene, from approximately 1904, shows the pub (last building to the right of the parked tram), alongside Victorian cottages dating from the 1860s. To the left is the old yeoman's cottage, 1660, the oldest building of the village. Although the pub is a Victorian structure built to complement the rural surrounds of the village, an earlier inn would have existed on the site. Heywood's memorial, shown to the left of the tram, was the site of the ancient chapel of West Derby, thought to have been in existence since Saxon times and demolished circa 1860.

Richard Rawlinson, a well-known Liverpool figure during the 19th century, took over the premises in approximately 1850, and remained until his death in 1888. He was considered to be a lively character of great wit and humour. After his death, his widow continued to run the business until 1894. For a period of just over 30 years, from 1908 until the early 1940s, the manager was John Barry, whose surname became, and still is, the nickname of the pub, Barry's.

We can gain an insight into the drinking habits of over 100 years ago from the following conversation between Richard Rawlinson and a customer concerning a new licensing law of the time, regarding Sunday drinking. It was reported in the *Liverpool Citizen* in the 1880s: 'It's a scandalous interference with a man's liberty in a free country like this,' said the convivial landlord, 'to punish a man for getting a drop too much. Why Sir, it's treating drunkenness as a crime and it's no such thing, Sir; it's a privilege! It's one of the things that distinguishes man from the lower animals!' Then, alluding to the effect of alcohol on health, 'Why! Sir, good liquor never killed anybody yet! I have known dozens of men in this very village who have come to this house regularly, day after day for some years past, some of 'em are in this room tonight, and they're all well and hearty. I've known others that were teetotallers, they're dead Sir; all dead!'

Another pub of the village was the Royal Oak, which was demolished in the 1950s to make way for a row of shops. The final pub, the Sefton Arms, is open to date and has always been a thriving establishment. It was included in a list of the principal hotels in Liverpool, and its environs, as long ago as 1855.

The Old Derby Arms

In the backgound of this 1998 shot can be seen the demolition of Winterburn Heights. Modern pubs, unlike the old corner locals, were built to accommodate the shift in population and were large spacious establishments mainly in their own grounds, although fewer and further between, this one is located in West Derby.

Although now long-established, many of the then modern suburban pubs were built over earlier structures which had served rural communities, sometimes for centuries. Three examples of this are the following:

The Greyhound

The Greyhound in Knotty Ash, close to West Derby, is one such pub built in the early 1930s. This view of the original is from 1924, when the licensee was James Clement Dudley (standing by the door). Note the Brewer's name on the gable-end, whose Brewery was located close to the pub in Knotty Ash. In fact, the building still remains, although it is no longer a Brewery.

Dog and Gun

The current pub dates from 1928 and, like the latter, replaced an earlier pub shown in this view. Originally listed in Croxteth Hall Lane, West Derby, the premises is now at number 1 Carr Lane East. This view is from the 1920s, shortly before demolition to make way for the present pub. The houses shown have also been demolished and replaced by modern housing.

Sefton Arms Hotel

Currently listed at number 4 Carr Lane East, this view is from approximately 1908, when listed in Carr Lane. The name is clearly displayed with Wine and Spirits written in the window and the licensee, Alfred W Warn. The current pub replaced this one in the 1930s. It was renamed the Sportsman but has since reverted to its original name.